BRITISH INTERIOR HOUSE STYLES

AN EASY REFERENCE GUIDE

Trevor Yorke

COUNTRYSIDE BOOKS

First published 2012
© Trevor Yorke 2012

COUNTRYSIDE BOOKS
3 Catherine Road
Newbury, Berkshire

To view our complete range of books,
please visit us at
www.countrysidebooks.co.uk

ISBN 978 1 84674 300 9

Illustrations by the author

Designed by Peter Davies, Nautilus Design
Produced through MRM Associates Ltd., Reading
Typeset by CJWT Solutions, St Helens
Printed by Information Press, Oxford

CONTENTS

INTRODUCTION   4

Chapter 1
TUDOR AND JACOBEAN STYLES 1500–1660   6

Chapter 2
RESTORATION AND QUEEN ANNE STYLES 1660–1720   12

Chapter 3
EARLY GEORGIAN STYLES 1720–1760   18

Chapter 4
MID GEORGIAN STYLES 1760–1800   26

Chapter 5
REGENCY STYLES 1800–1840   35

Chapter 6
EARLY VICTORIAN STYLES 1840–1880   45

Chapter 7
LATE VICTORIAN AND EDWARDIAN STYLES 1880–1920   56

Chapter 8
INTER AND POST WAR STYLES 1920–1960   67

GLOSSARY   76

TIMECHART   78

INDEX   79

Introduction

The interior of a period house can reflect more than the style of its last make over. The richly figured oak panels of a timber-framed hall, the graceful and delicate plasterwork of a Georgian drawing room or the intense colour and clutter of a Victorian terrace have, in their fixtures and fittings, clues to the character, ambition and taste of previous occupants. The form of the room, its position within the house and the shape of its finer details can help to unravel the development and original date of interior spaces. Unlike the exterior of the house, where the huge expense of major changes limited drastic updating, the interior was prone to regular redecoration and fitting out with fashionable new furnishings, sometimes creating an eclectic mix of old and new, or completely covering up earlier details.

Underlying the bewildering range of styles and the whims of individual householders are some general changes in form, materials and fashions which can help the untrained eye to recognise the age and period of a room and some of its furnishings and fittings. It might be the type of wood used, the profile of a cornice or the colours in a wallpaper that give a clue to when that piece was first fitted. There are also small details which can help identify original parts from the wealth of imitation and reinserted furnishings and fittings which our predecessors especially in the 19th century were all too keen to use. For instance, old oak wall panelling was often removed and fitted into new

properties but with little attention paid to the finer details of its construction. So, the flat chamfer which was always along the bottom edge of original pieces to make dusting easier can be found up the side or along the top where it has been moved. In this book, it is these general themes and characteristic details which are focused upon to empower the reader to recognise the popular styles and the period in which they were applied.

By using over 200 individual colour drawings and black and white sketches, the book illustrates the changing face of domestic interiors and introduces the key styles of fixtures and fittings over the past 500 years. Each chapter covers a consecutive period and works from examples of complete rooms down to details like furniture and lighting, with the accompanying captions highlighting the details and giving additional clues to look out for. Whether you would just like to know the background to the period houses you visit, want to know more about an old house you own or are trying to recreate or restore an historic interior, this book will provide an easy-to-follow introduction to the subject.

Before we race back 500 years, it is worth noting the limits of cramming so much history into such a short space. For simplicity, the dates of each chapter have been rounded up; therefore they do not mark the exact date of a change of monarch or style. Illustrations are used to include numerous important aspects of a style; as a result only a few of the drawings are of actual rooms but are rather suggestions of what they may have looked like. With the earlier periods, most of what we know comes from pattern books, illustrations and writings, less so from actual discoveries, so the colours and designs used show how an interior may have appeared rather than a definite scheme.

It is also important to remember when looking through this book or visiting a house over a couple of hundred years old that, on the whole, what you are looking at are the homes of the better-off members of a community, who even at the beginning of the 20th century represented less than a quarter of the population. What we regard today as a narrow terrace or Tudor timber-framed cottage was in its day an imposing house of a successful merchant or yeoman farmer. Few of the single storey houses which the majority of the working population lived in before the Industrial Age have survived, and most of the poor quality terraces which housed them during the Victorian period were swept away during 20th-century redevelopments. Their interiors would have been quite Spartan, with very few possessions, and it was not until mass production and cheaper materials from the late 19th century that style would have become an issue in their homes.

It was the gentry who were the trend-setters of their day, with a class below of professionals, merchants and farmers who emulated the latest fashions, those in cosmopolitan areas in the following years, others in more remote parts in the following decades. As this book focuses upon the buildings which you can visit or own, the earliest interiors which are featured will be from houses of the wealthy; by the second half of the 18th century it will include those of middle-class professionals; but only when it reaches the late Victorian period will it be representative of a wider proportion of the population.

Trevor Yorke

FIG 0.1: *A living room with labels of key elements of the interior.*

Chapter ❶

Tudor and Jacobean Styles

1500–1660

FIG 1.1: *An Elizabethan interior from a luxurious urban house, with the owner's wealth displayed in the oak wall panelling, elaborate fireplace and decorative plastered ceiling. Furniture was limited but wall hangings, bold fabrics and splashes of paint made the finest rooms colourful places.*

Our journey through the history of English house interiors begins some 500 years ago when Henry VIII had recently ascended the throne. Over the following century and a half, up to the end of the Commonwealth in 1660, our domestic surroundings had begun a transformation from one based around a communal open hall to an arrangement of private rooms separated from the owner's household. This key change was already underway at gentry level when we join the story and was still taking place lower down the social scale at the end of this period. A key element was the adoption of the fireplace and chimney set in a side wall, as opposed to the previous variety of arrangements where the hearth was within the body of the room. This change enabled a floor to be inserted above the old open hall, usually forming a great chamber in the largest houses where the family could take their meals and entertain guests; while the household who had formerly shared this daily routine were now relegated to the old hall below. In the smaller homes of the merchant or yeoman farmer this two-storey plan, with bedrooms above a living room and parlour, was widely adopted; in some wealthy areas like the wool rich Suffolk towns, this happened from the beginning of this period, whilst elsewhere it became common from the later 1500s as rising incomes sparked a 'Great Rebuilding' of houses.

The interior of Early Tudor houses was very much a continuation of late medieval themes, with little concern for the overall form of the room, and style being limited to decorative elements like tapestries. This was a time when the gentry regularly moved from one property to another, taking not only chests full of belongings but also removing the windows and taking these with them too. Glass was still a luxury product at this time and windows only became fixed from 1579 onwards. During this period, however, the Renaissance on the Continent began to influence our Gothic isle and houses at the top end of the market began to have symmetrical façades and rooms behind to match. Staircases which had been little more than ladders to access upper rooms in the medieval period now became a more impressive feature of the house, although they were usually enclosed in a tower or to the side of the building. The exposed beams of the floor above began to be covered over and patterned ceilings formed in plaster. Walls, doorways and furniture could now be covered with patterns copied from illustrations of the latest Classical styles (often from the Protestant Netherlands), as columns, capitals and

FIG 1.2: *The vast majority of the population lived in the country and would have been familiar with interiors like this example from a 16th-century farmhouse. An inglenook fireplace, straw strewn on a beaten earth floor and low beamed ceilings were characteristic of this period. The cupboard to the left of the fire was built into the wall to store spices, salt or other valuables.*

pediments began replacing the pointed arch as the key decorative components for the next 300 years. At this date masons and carpenters applied these details with little knowledge of the rules of Classical architecture so they can appear as rather clumsy, with deeply carved masses of detail, especially in the Elizabethan period (1559–1603).

In the more modest middle-class home this transition took longer and, although owners did copy the fashions set by their social superiors, they were often adapted by local craftsmen into regional styles. Most farmhouses generally had ceilings which were beamed; walls panelled in the finest rooms or painted with

decorative scenes, patterns or scripts; floors covered with rushes to gather up the dirt; and with an inglenook fireplace as the focal point of the living room and parlour. The houses of the wealthier merchant or farmer by the end of this period could have featured plastered

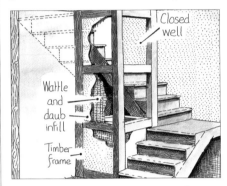

FIG 1.4: Closed well staircase: *In larger houses the stairs could be more spacious and built around a central well which was closed off with wattle and daub or timber panelling. It was common for this otherwise wasted space to have cupboards inserted.*

FIG 1.3: Winder stairs: *As the better-off built themselves new houses of two or more storeys so they needed a staircase. In most Tudor homes these were simple types like this winder stair and were commonly found tucked into a corner beside a fire or in a separate tower attached to the exterior. These were plain utilitarian structures with little opportunity for decoration.*

FIG 1.5: Splat balusters: *In the early 17th century carved balusters became more common, a cheaper version being one cut from a flat plank of timber called a splat baluster. The acorn finial on top of the post was a popular form in the late Elizabethan and Jacobean periods.*

ceilings, more extensive panelling and furniture carved in the latest Classical styles. One point worth making is that despite the rather plain appearance today of Tudor and Jacobean homes, they originally would have been more colourful places; the black and white treatment is a later Victorian interpretation.

FIG 1.6: Open stairwell: *In the finest houses of the Elizabethan and Jacobean period an open staircase with carved balusters (A) and newel posts (B) became a feature for display, albeit still enclosed off to the side of the principal rooms. Woodwork and furniture often had details picked out in bright colours as here.*

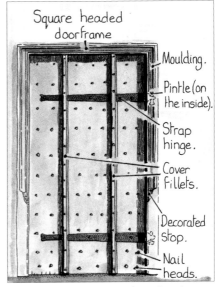

FIG 1.7: Doors: *Most external and internal doors of the period were made from vertical planks of uneven width, held together with battens across their inner face (they closed flat onto the back of the doorway and were not recessed within it). The finest could have decorative ironwork and wooden fillets.*

FIG 1.8: Fireplaces: *These could range from simple timber beam lintels above a large opening (see Fig 1.2,) up to fine stone surrounds with shallow pointed arches and highly decorative wooden or plaster overmantels as in this example (see also Fig 1.1). Wood was the most common fuel although coal was imported to some cities.*

FIG 1.9: Ceilings: *Tudor ceilings were usually no more than the exposed joists and central bridging beam of the floor above. The edges were usually chamfered (if found today with sharp edges, then it was probably originally intended to be covered) and, on the finest, moulded edges and decorative bosses were added for effect.*

FIG 1.10: Plaster ceilings: *From the late 16th century plaster ceilings with deep geometric patterns (as in these examples) and drooping pendants (see Fig 1.1) were fitted in the finest rooms.*

FIG 1.11: Linenfold panelling: *In the early Tudor period oak panels with a pattern which looked like folded linen were popular in the best houses.*

FIG 1.12: Square panelling: *From the mid 16th century plain square panelling becomes popular, with moulded edges around the top and sides (A) and a plain chamfer along the bottom (B). Flat, geometric patterns known as strapwork (C) were distinctive of the period from 1580–1620.*

FIG 1.13: Chairs: *These were rare in the 16th century, usually reserved for the head of the table (hence the term 'chairman'), but became more common by the early 17th century. Tudor types tended to be boxy (left), with a loose cushion fixed by string on some examples. By the Jacobean period they had become more open, with turned legs and arm supports and decorative crests on the back. Fitted upholstery was rare at this date. Yorkshire and Derbyshire chairs were local types which had open backs with two horizontal rails across, often with arched designs carved on them. Inlaid patterns formed with different woods (right) were popular in the late 16th and 17th centuries.*

FIG 1.14: Tables: *In the early Tudor period, tables were often simple trestle types with benches and stools. It was only from the Elizabethan period that finer carved pieces could be more readily found. This example has the distinctive bulbous acorns on the legs, with stretch rails close to the floor and strapwork designs along the top rail. Jacobean tables had more elegant legs with columns and capitals and less decorative carving, a general rule which applied to all furniture in this later period.*

FIG 1.15: Chests: *Open buffets to display dinner ware (see Fig 1.1) and chests with doors (and drawers by the Jacobean period) were a common feature in the finest rooms. In the 16th century they would usually have richly-carved surfaces but by the 17th century they become plainer, with decoration being formed by geometric patterns in the panelling as in this example.*

FIG 1.16: Beds: *The four-poster bed, with the bedstead recessed behind the front posts or linked into it as in this example, was the most distinctive feature of bedrooms in this period. The narrow arched decoration along the edge of the canopy and the semi circular arches on the panels are distinctive of late Elizabethan and Jacobean woodwork.*

Chapter ❷

Restoration and Queen Anne Styles

1660–1720

FIG 2.1: *A principal reception room at the turn of the 18th century which displays the fashion for continental styles and the taste for luxury in the finest houses. By the early 1700s homes of merchants, lawyers and other professionals could also be found with similar furnishings to those purchased by the upper classes as they became aware of these fashions.*

The reigns of Charles II, William and Mary and Queen Anne bore witness to some of the most significant changes in domestic architec- ture, in part influenced by the monarchs themselves. When Charles was restored to the throne in 1660 after more than a decade of Puritan rule he brought with him a taste for a new Classical style from his time spent in the Netherlands and France. His queen also introduced elements from her Portuguese homeland and her dowry included the possession of Bombay, an important trading post with the Far East which, in this period, began a fascination with Chinese and Japanese decoration and ornaments.

This introduction of continental and exotic styles in fashionable urban areas came at the same time as the Great Fire of London of 1666 changed the way houses were built. Although a few designers, most notably Inigo Jones, had developed an understanding of the Classical rules regarding symmetry, form and proportion before the Civil War, most had simply applied columns and

arches onto buildings which were shaped by the client's requirements and local tradition. Now, in the wake of the fire, the rebuilding of London was carried out within strict regulations. The width of street, the size of the house and the materials it was made from were controlled by inspectors. A new form of Classically-inspired terrace, often built by speculative builders and leased out, now reshaped the Capital and began influencing other towns and cities.

There were equally dramatic changes inside the house. Formerly, even the largest houses had only been one room deep and had just been wrapped around a courtyard to appear larger. Now, double pile houses (two rooms deep) became the norm for the finer detached house and urban terrace. Rooms which in the past had been accessed by passing

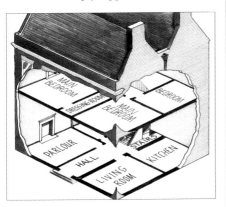

FIG 2.2: Double pile house: *A cut-away view of a large, late 17th-century house, showing how the double pile structure and the central hall permitted direct access into each room for increased privacy. The staircase was now sited in a more prominent position; in this case at the rear of the hall while the kitchen and storage rooms could be incorporated at the back of the house.*

FIG 2.3: Carving: *This was the period in which wood carving came to the fore, especially in the hands of masters like Grinling Gibbons. Decoration included fruits, flowers and, in this balustrade, intertwined leaves. The cherub or angel figure (as here with its back against the newel post) could be found on finer pieces, some with a crown possibly celebrating the Restoration.*

through one to another now had passages linking them, allowing people to enter without being noticed by those in adjoining rooms, a further step towards greater privacy. Classical proportions and symmetry were applied to the interior, with carefully planned features and fittings, and new vertical windows (from the 1680s available with sliding sashes) of regular size and spacing which allowed greater light into a room.

The hall was now relegated to a narrow passage behind the entrance which in these new deeper houses had no windows illuminating it so a squat over-light was fitted above the door; later types with ironwork patterns being referred to as fanlights. Two principal rooms either side of this, with service rooms at the rear and bedrooms above became the basic plan for Classical detached houses. In the more restricted urban terrace the first floor was often reserved for the most important reception room as the hall below narrowed the width of the adjacent room.

Those who wished to copy the style set by the monarch had to import much of the goods they required. Skilled

FIG 2.4: Doors: *Panelled doors became common in fashionable homes and they typically have two large panels with one, two, or three small panels inserted between them as in this example. Plank and batten types were still widely used in service areas and in rural properties. Bolection moulding, with the highest raised part closest to the centre (see Fig 2.5) was used around the door panels in the late 17th and early 18th centuries.*

FIG 2.5: Fireplaces: *Fashionable fireplaces now had deep bolection moulding made in wood or stone, surrounding the opening which would often be integrated into the panelling across the wall. This bolection moulding with its deepest part closest to the opening was widely used on door surrounds and fireplaces from the 1670s to 1720s. Cast-iron fire backs, often with the royal coat of arms, were popular throughout the 17th century.*

Protestants fleeing persecution in France and Dutch craftsmen who came over with William, however, helped establish the manufacture of fine-quality fashionable furnishings and fabrics in England by the end of the period. The Baroque style dominated with luxurious and exuberant fittings, polished walnut or lacquered furniture and heavenly scenes painted on ceilings creating space and movement. However, the majority of the lesser gentry and middle classes still had their rural properties fitted out in more traditional forms. In the country, oak still dominated furniture and fittings, shaped by a mix of vernacular styles and classical decoration or being puritanically plain in form. It would not be until the next period that the Classical styles would be more generally accepted.

FIG 2.6: Ceilings: *Plaster ceilings became common in the better class of house although they were still rather low at this date except in the finest reception rooms. In these grand show pieces, large panelled sections with deep oval surrounds featuring plastered patterns or painted scenes were distinctive of this Baroque period. Beams are often found exposed in houses of this period as later owners desired a rustic appearance. However, if the underside of the joists line up with that of the main beams, then it is likely that it was originally plastered.*

FIG 2.7: Staircases: *The staircase was now a prominent feature and open well types, with carved or turned balusters and decorated newel posts with recessed panels (see Fig 2.3) were distinctive of the age. The balusters were usually turned, with vase shapes (right) and bottle shapes popular, and the unturned sections top and bottom being quite short. Twisted balusters (left) were a fashion which came over with Charles II's Portuguese queen and remained a popular decorative form into the early 1700s (the balusters resting upon the side piece being called a closed string). Splat balusters were still fitted copying the style of turned types and now having pierced decoration in the middle of some. The newel post often had a finial fitted on top, sometimes with a matching pendant hanging down from the flight above.*

FIG 2.8: Panelling: *Wooden wall panelling remained fashionable, now with large upper sections as in this example. By the turn of the 18th century imported softwoods (often referred to as deal) was being used in houses; this less attractive material either being painted in stone colours (see Fig 2.1), green, cream or browns, or was grained to look like a finer wood. By this time dado rails and skirting boards were often added to protect the panelling from the backs of chairs which could now be found positioned against walls.*

Fig 2.9: Gate-leg tables: *It became fashionable in the late 17th and early 18th centuries to dine at a number of smaller tables, and round gate-leg types as in this example with twisted legs are distinctive of the period (some also had drawers fitted).*

Fig 2.10: Long case clocks: *With the introduction of pendulums in the mid 17th century the long case clock became a fashionable possession for the wealthiest men and, by the early 18th century, were common in the finest houses (they only became known as grandfather clocks after the 1878 song My Grandfather's Clock by Henry Clay Work). Another piece of furniture which appeared in this period was the bookcase, usually with glass-fronted doors, now that printed books were more widely available and collected by gentlemen of taste.*

Fig 2.11: Mirrors: *Before 1618 Venetian craftsmen had a monopoly on making the plate glass used in mirrors and it was only with foreign know-how that the technique to make them was introduced here after this date. Production was stepped up after the Restoration and mirrors with elaborate carved and gilded frames were popular in the better class of home. Another popular finish to the frame was japanning which was an imitation of Japanese lacquered finishes with, in this example, a black polished surface. It often featured scenes from Japanese life and was popular on furniture from the 1680s to the 1720s.*

Fig 2.12: Side tables: *Small tables used for playing card games, writing, or taking tea became popular with the wealthy in the second half of the 17th century. This example in fashionable walnut has twisted legs and an interlocking stretcher between the four uprights, a distinctive feature of this period. It also shows how*

Restoration furniture could be colourful and decorative, with marquetry (patterns created on the surface from different coloured woods) being revived in this period. Early examples tend to have small areas of decoration. By William and Mary's time, though, immigrant Dutch craftsmen had introduced finer quality work which tends to cover the whole surface of the furniture and often features flowers in the patterns.

FIG 2.13: Restoration chairs: *The finest chairs in the first half of this period tend to have exuberant carving and turned*

uprights, with the stretchers between the front legs matching the design of the rail across the top of the back. Scrolled legs were also popular as in this example. The seat and back often contained caning which remained a fashionable material for chairs until the early 18th century.

FIG 2.14: Oak chairs: *In rural areas, oak was still widely used and chairs with two cross rails between the uprights often with arches and an arcade of turned supports, as in this example, were popular in northern counties.*

FIG 2.15: Queen Anne chairs: *By the early 18th century the backs of chairs*

had become narrower, stretchers between the legs were omitted, the top rail ran across the uprights rather than between them and cabriole legs, with their distinctive knee shape, were introduced, as in this example. Fixed upholstery often in blue, black or red velvet was also becoming widespread. This simplified design with its single curved splat up the back is typical of a style which would become widespread in the following Georgian period.

Chapter ❸

Early Georgian Styles

1720–1760

FIG 3.1: A mid 18th-century drawing room. *This had grown from a small space used after a meal to become the principal reception room in the house, a feminine domain with light-coloured walls and an airy feel. It was still flexible at this date with chairs and furniture which could be grouped in the centre or pushed back up against the walls when not in use. Note that the dado and cornice are painted the same colour as the panelling.*

Since the Restoration in 1660 there had been a number of concessions from the Crown to Parliament such that, by the time a Protestant successor to the childless Queen Anne had been found in Hanover and its Protector was crowned George I, Parliament had gained power and influence. Rather than being called upon only when the monarch required money, Parliament now had a regular sitting from autumn through to spring, and a social 'Season' developed when the M.P.s and their entourage descended upon London. Most of these aristocrats and the gentry now had a large town house in addition to their country seat in order to enjoy the pleasures of the Capital and to entertain and accommodate an increasing number of guests. This encouraged them to make these urban properties as grand and tasteful as their country houses and those of the middle classes who were still subservient to the monarchy and aristocrats tried to emulate the latest styles they introduced. As a result the Early Georgian period saw rapid growth in London which was enhanced further by the new civil servants, now appointed on merit rather than favour, and an increasing number of professionals, tradesmen and servants to serve these classes.

In the 18th century an understanding of Classical literature and architecture was the hallmark of a gentleman of good taste and many of the upper classes sent their first son off on a Grand Tour of Europe, principally to visit Italy, as the final part of their education. The craze for rebuilding or extending country houses in this period was partly due to young gentlemen wishing to display their new-found skills in design and to house the crate loads of artefacts they had brought back with them. While they were abroad the second son was often given an ecclesiastical education and upon gaining his own parish usually set about building a grand new vicarage with a priority on entertaining those of his class rather than serving his parishioners.

This wealth of new urban terraces, rural mansions and stout vicarages was shaped by a new Palladian style in which the Classical orders as reinterpreted by the 16th-century Italian architect

Palladio were strictly applied without the exuberant garnish of the previous Baroque and a tendency in the largest houses for style to have preference over convenience (kitchens could be so far from dining rooms that the food became cold before it arrived at the table). However, inside, flamboyant decoration was still in favour and in the finest houses developed into the Rococo during the 1740s and '50s, with incredibly florid displays of swirling plasterwork and carving. Chinoiserie, a Chinese style applied to Western objects, was popular during the 18th century, and was promoted by the leading furniture designer of his day, Thomas Chippendale. He, along with other

FIG 3.2: *Cut-away view of a mid 18th-century, middle-class terrace, with the service rooms in the basement. In this more modest house the principal bedroom is on the taller first floor and the family rooms on the ground.*

FIG 3.3: Bedrooms: *In the finest 17th-century houses these had often been on the ground floor at one end of a suite of rooms running along the rear (the enfilade) where the owner could receive guests. During the 18th century, however, it could be either on the piano nobile behind the drawing room or a more private space on an upper floor. In these days before bathrooms, the bedroom was used for washing and dressing, as well as for sleeping. Four-poster beds were still common, many with upholstered, full-height headboards and heavy fabrics around the outside to keep draughts out, as in this example. Furniture was not such a priority as the bedroom became more private so older pieces from reception rooms were often moved here when they were being updated. In large houses there would usually be an adjoining room, a boudoir for the lady (from the French verb 'bouder' meaning 'to sulk') and a closet or cabinet for the gentleman. (The closest ministers to the king would often meet him in such a room, hence the term 'Cabinet' used today for the principal ministers in government).*

leading architects and craftsmen, published pattern books which helped establish new styles and design with a fashion-hungry wealthy clientele.

The gradual separation of the family from what was now less of a household and more a hierarchy of servants continued during the early 18th century, with most urban terraces now having the kitchen and a scullery or back kitchen sited in a full-depth basement.

FIG 3.4: Kitchens: *A basement kitchen from a large 18th-century terraced house. The open fire was used for roasting, with spits operated in this example by a smokejack (a fan above the fire which turned as the heat and smoke rose). Fire grates were common by 1700 and side ovens as pictured here appeared in the 1750s and were the first crude ranges. A central table for preparation and dressers for pots, pans and everyday crockery were standard fittings. Behind the kitchen there would usually be a smaller back kitchen or scullery where the washing could take place. Water was brought in from a well, pump or, occasionally, supplied in wooden pipes where there was a mains supply. A copper (a metal pot encased in brick with a fire below) was used for heating it.*

Rather than entering through the main door, the staff could climb down the steps in the area at the front which permitted light and air to enter these subterranean spaces. There was also a change in the nature of the rooms as they progressively became less flexible and had a more defined role. Therefore, in addition to the dining and drawing room, the principal reception rooms, there could be a library, important for social status even if the books were just for show, and a morning or breakfast room, usually at the front of the house for light meals and pleasure pursuits. In some houses a parlour was still used (in modest homes it was in place of the drawing room) as somewhere private for the family to retire to.

FIG 3.6: Windows: *Sash windows with internal shutters were common, as in this example, being split horizontally into two or three sections so the upper part could be opened for light while the lower parts protected delicate furnishings from the sun. Roller and Venetian blinds could also be found from the turn of the 18th century.*

FIG 3.5: Doors: *Those in the main rooms now usually had six panels, a small upper, larger centre and slightly shorter*

bottom one, with the panels raised in the centre (fielded). If it was made from a good-quality wood, then it would have been polished; any other type would have been painted or grained. Handles were popular in the early 18th century, knobs becoming the norm later on.

FIG 3.7: Stairs: *Open string staircases, where the balusters rest upon the top of each tread and there is no string up the side, became popular during this period. The balusters were usually grouped in twos or threes and had small decorative brackets fitted under each tread. In the finest houses the stairs might be pushed to one side to make space for a magnificent hall.*

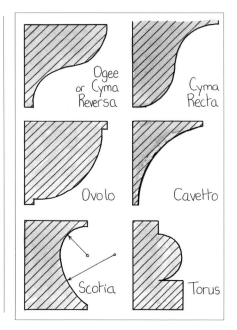

FIG 3.8: *Balusters became more slender, with longer unturned sections top and bottom than in the previous period, with vase shapes (left), columns set on a squat urn (centre) and barley twist (right) being popular forms.*

FIG 3.9: Mouldings: *Cornices, dado rails and the mouldings around panels and doors used in Georgian and Regency houses can look rather complex at first but can usually be broken down into simple elements as shown here (ogee, ovolo and egg and dart were popular in this period).*

FIG 3.10: Wallcoverings: *Panelling was still fitted in principal rooms but usually only on the lower part of the wall, with the section above plastered and, in the finest houses, covered by damasks, velvets, silks, tapestry and even leather. Hand-made wallpaper was used as a cheaper alternative to fabric hangings, with designs copying those on curtains, upholstery and tapestries, and even incorrporating details like stitching and lace. They could range from simple repeated patterns to flock papers imitating velvet, floral designs (left and centre), and*

Chinese landscapes (right). They were not pasted up at this date but fixed to a linen background and then hung on battens or pinned to the wall with copper tacks. Popular colours in this period for panelling and wall coverings included greens (sage, olive and a lighter grey type), blue-grey, straw-yellow and stone colours. It was still usual to paint the whole room in one colour (including mouldings) although later in the period dark brown became commonly used for the doors and skirtings.

FIG 3.11: Fireplaces: *Stone, marble and wooden surrounds were now planted onto the wall rather than being an integral part of panelling or a lintel holding up the structure. Bolection types gave way to Classical designs, early 18th-century ones often having side projections towards the top (eared) while lavish Rococo types with a curvaceous profile could be found in the 1740s and '50s.*

FIG 3.12: Furniture: *Mahogany becomes popular during this period, partly due to the dropping of import duties on timber from America in 1721, overtaking walnut as the timber for fashionable pieces by the 1730s. The simple structures of the Queen Anne period are more heavily decorated during this time as Classical architectural features are added, like the broken pediment on top of this bookcase, to create monumental pieces which can overwhelm rooms. Bookcases were given this treatment to reflect the importance of books, or at least the possession of them, as the library or study at the rear of the ground floor reflected the owner's taste and Classical education. In addition to these glass-fronted bookcases, there might also have been a lectern on which to display a notable manuscript, a writing desk and paintings to inspire conversation with guests.*

FIG 3.13: Chests: *A chest-upon-chest or two-stage tallboy was popular in bedrooms during this period as in this example. Lower two- or three-drawer chests known as commodes became fashionable from the 1740s (it would only be used as a term for chamber pot later in the 19th century). Another popular piece which took on its familiar form in this period was the writing bureau, its sloping, hinged desk covering up a wealth of compartments and secret drawers (often hidden by pilasters up the sides) which the Georgians loved.*

FIG 3.14: Side tables: *Games and card tables were an important feature in principal rooms at a time when low light made other pastimes impractical. The game of cards was a desired social skill and could be taught by gaming masters. The tables had cabriole legs so no stretchers were needed between to get in the way, and the tops could be unfolded by a variety of mechanisms when they were needed. Other side tables could have real or fake marble tops, a popular surface in this period.*

FIG 3.15: *A Rococo-style mirror, with its characteristic asymmetrical swirling foliage. It was known as 'French taste' at the time; the term 'Rococo' was applied later, named after the rocky grottos which were popular in this period.*

FIG 3.16: Dining tables: *In the dining room, gate-leg tables were still popular, usually oval or round, with square ones, which could be pushed together to make a longer piece, introduced later in the period. As with other pieces of furniture the cabriole leg was often used, as in this example, freeing up more space beneath, although twisted and vase-shaped legs were also popular. There would also be a cabinet for serving drinks and a sideboard for food, while a dado and skirting ran around the strong-coloured walls as it was still customary to move the table and chairs to the edge of the room when they had been finished with.*

FIG 3.17: Chippendale: *Thomas Chippendale was the most influential authority on furniture design in the middle of the 18th century. He produced the first pattern book dedicated to furniture and through it promoted his designs which were notable for integrating aspects of various styles while maintaining a quality of craftsmanship, practicality and grace. In general, his chairs tend to be squarer than earlier pieces, often with straight legs as in this Chinoiserie-style piece with its distinctive open fretwork back. Most of the pieces referred to today as Chippendale were produced by others based on his designs.*

FIG 3.18: *A Rococo-style upholstered chair. The carved timber could be painted white and gilded, this combination being distinctive of some of the finest interiors in the mid 18th century.*

FIG 3.19: Chairs: *In the 16th and early 17th centuries, chairs had been a luxury item with most people using benches and stools. By the 18th century, however, they were commonplace: ranging from richly upholstered or flamboyant Rococo pieces in large urban houses to simple oak chairs in rural areas. The most fashionable versions tended to have arms which curve outwards, with the ends of some formed into an eagle or animal head and later a simple scroll. Cabriole legs with claw and ball feet were common but straight legs came into fashion in the 1750s. The backs still had hooped tops and concave splats in the early years (left), some with a rail just below the top, but later the whole piece becomes more square with a top rail shaped like Cupid's bow and the splat pierced with patterns (right).*

Chapter ❹

Mid Georgian Styles

1760–1800

FIG 4.1: A late 18th-century dining room. *During this period, rooms began to take on their more familiar form, as in this example, where the table was now a fixed piece of furniture in the centre of the room. In the finest rooms architects also formed alcoves behind partitions of columns and arched niches for statues, while walls and ceilings could be adorned with pattern in distinctive shallow and delicate mouldings.*

The second half of the 18th century marks a sudden upturn in the population, especially in London, and the beginning of the transition of the country from an agrarian dominated economy to one based around industry. Improved road transport, new canals and developments in steam engines helped establish larger-scale mills and factories and at the same time brought the cost of coal down so it became available to urban households. Speculative-built houses were being erected not only to meet the huge demand from the Capital but also in new industrial cities, expanding ports, and fashionable spa towns like Bath and Buxton. Much of this new building was for an emerging middle class, a growing number of people who were making a healthy living out of increased trade around the world, booming industries, mining and quarrying and the professionals who served those who could afford their services or products.

The owners and tenants of these symmetrical detached houses and tall urban terraces (the vast majority were rented out) sought to emulate the fashionable interiors of their social superiors, ones which were still shaped by Classical orders but now inspired by new studies of Ancient Greece rather than just Rome. The most influential designers who grasped the decorative possibilities of this new source were the Adam brothers. They replaced heavy Palladian features with new graceful and delicate forms of Classical detailing, with distinctive shallow mouldings, lighter colours and more freedom to decorate surfaces. They also promoted the idea of designing the house as a whole, so whereas in the previous period you could have a refined Palladian façade with lively Rococo fittings in the rooms, they would create decorative schemes and pieces of furniture which complemented the style of the exterior.

In areas where this building boom occurred, regulations were not tight enough to cut out bad practices and just as render could cover up the use of cheap bricks on the outside walls so a general acceptance of sham materials meant wood could be painted to look like marble; a mix of size, resin and whiting could imitate wood; and cheap mouldings could appear to be hand-carved. Even the Adam brothers were happy to paint furniture and fittings.

Although these new Classical styles dominated the interior, there were other sources of inspiration, most notably Chinese designs which remained popular for furniture and wallpapers and a new Gothick style (with a 'k' at the end to differentiate it from later Victorian Gothic) with the pointed arch appearing in chair backs and furnishing patterns. Some of these exotic and historic sources will often be found mixed up in the same design.

The arrangement of rooms within most houses remained much the same as that which had developed through the previous period. In larger houses a separate music room could be added as

FIG 4.2: Dining room: *As the table became a fixed piece in the centre of the room, the dado was often replaced by a picture rail for hanging paintings which the gentlemen in this male-dominated room could admire. Sideboards with a low curtain and rail fitted on top were used for serving food. Tables were usually rectangular, some with semi-circular ends which could be separated to make side tables.*

27

FIG 4.3: Drawing room: *This remained the principal reception room, where afternoon tea could be taken now that it had become a fashionable practice from the mid 18th century. The room could be lavishly decorated as in this Adams' style example which has their distinctive shallow mouldings defining the wall panels and delicate ornamental designs within them. This arrangement was formed from plaster either hand-moulded on site or made up of pre-moulded pieces bought from workshops and set into the final coat of plaster,*

replacing wooden wall panelling which had been popular over the previous centuries. The Adams usually painted the surrounding walls in a light pink, blue or green, while mirrors had narrow, delicate gilded frames.

it became fashionable to entertain guests with a modest concert. In the dining room the table became a fixed feature in the centre while the drawing room, where the new fashion for taking afternoon tea could take place, remained a more flexible space (hence the dado rail was retained). Upstairs there was a general relaxation in the separation of the sexes. In the finest houses, double doors linked male and female apartments.

FIG 4.4: *Columns or pilasters (flat versions attached to walls or furniture) were often used in the interior during this period. They could be fitted to define an alcove (see Fig 4.1), to divide up a room and make its proportions more balanced, or were used as decorative details on furniture, fireplaces and door cases. The panels within a room and on doors were arranged to reflect the proportions of a temple from the Ancient World, with the lower section the solid base on which it stood, the tall centre part the column, and the short upper section the entablature which comprised the architrave and cornice. The proportions varied between the different Classical orders and these were characterised by the decorative capital at the top of each column. (Above, from left to right) The Roman orders Corinthian, Doric and Ionic had been used since the late 16th century whilst Ancient Greek versions, Ionic and Doric, became popular by the end of the 18th century.*

FIG 4.5: Fireplaces: *Adam-style surrounds which are distinctive of this period typically had a central, rectangular plaque above the opening, a band of decorative detail below a mantleshelf which was deeper than earlier types (but not as deep as later Victorian versions) and, in the finest examples, a pair of figures or columns up the sides. Marble was still the stone of choice, either in white or with coloured pieces inserted into a plain background, while other materials could be painted to appear like it. Overmantels, which had been part of the structure of the surround and had remained popular into the 18th century, now fell from fashion, with a large mirror or painting hung from the wall usually taking its place. In rural areas, tiles had been used around the opening of more basic fireplaces; and the distinctive blue and white Delft tiles which had been popular in the 17th century and early 18th century were now replaced by home-produced versions.*

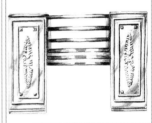

FIG 4.6: Grates: *Now that coal had become more widely available and cheaper, the grates which had formerly held logs had to be redesigned to contain the more compact lump which burnt best. Metal grates were produced with graceful silver-coloured polished fronts supported on pillars (brass was not common until the 19th century), balusters or legs (left and centre) and with the coal stacked in a narrow basket behind. There was little effort made at this date to improve the draw and efficiency of the fire. Although register grates which had an adjustable flap covering the entrance to the chimney stack had been invented, they did not become common until the following century. One advantage of the more compactly burning coal was the introduction of hob grates (right) which had a metal plate inserted to the side on which kettles and pans could boil water or keep food warm.*

FIG 4.7: Curtains: *Hanging fabric curtains covering the full window had become common in fashionable houses from the 1730s. Some were pulled up like a festoon blind while others were gathered into a top corner and draped down like swags. In the 1760s and '70s it became fashionable to have just one large curtain to one side to cover the window (left), this short-lived style being replaced by the more conventional 'French draw' with the fabric held on rings which slid along a rod, with window cornices or pelmets becoming popular too (right). The main curtain fabrics*

became lighter during this period. Cotton could not economically be produced in this country so Indian types were popular from the late 17th century (those from Calcutta becoming known here as calico) until a ban was enforced on importing to protect domestic manufacturers. They responded by making linen with block printed patterns to imitate the Indian fabric until Western cotton production became established in the 1770s, at first just in one colour but by 1790 with two or three (reds, blues, purple and black were commonly used). Chintz (a cotton with a glazed finish added to give it an attractive lustre and more resilience), with bold floral patterns and strongly-coloured calico, also became popular, with muslin (a loosely-woven and hence slightly transparent cotton fabric) as a sub curtain or net behind the main curtain. As the influence of the Adams' concept of designing the room as a whole became accepted so the idea of colour co-ordination between curtain fabrics, upholstery and wall coverings was introduced.

FIG 4.8: Ceilings: *Although most plastered ceilings were plain, the finest rooms could still have elaborate raised patterns but these were now much shallower and finer, with light pinks, lilacs and greens often used on the flat surfaces to help emphasise the design (some reflected the pattern of a rug on the floor in the same room). During this period the cornices covering the junction between the wall and ceiling became simpler and smaller than the rather strong architecturally-designed pieces from the early 18th century.*

FIG 4.9: Stairs: *Open string staircases with three balusters on each tread were widely fitted in this period. The balusters were similar to previous types but were thinner with longer, unturned lengths and simpler designs. Cast- and wrought-iron decorative balusters (as pictured here) which could be painted or gilded became fashionable in the finest houses from the 1760s.*

FIG 4.11: Floors: *Carpets which covered the complete floor could be found in some of the finer houses during the late 18th century but these were made from strips which were hand-sewn together on site making them an expensive and short-lived fashion. Rugs and large carpet pieces were now produced in this country: the most expensive from Axminster, and slightly cheaper ones from Wilton and Kidderminster. They could mirror the pattern in the ceiling (Fig 4.8) or pick up motifs used elsewhere in the room, reflecting the new ideas of coordinating design as in this example. Imported rugs and cheaper painted or oiled cloths were still used while the exposed floorboards were either painted dark brown or matched the colour of the wall woodwork.*

FIG 4.10 Wall treatment: *Wallpapers still reflected designs of fabrics (top right) with those featuring scenes from the landscape being popular in the 1760s and '70s (top left). Later in the period simpler designs became available (bottom left) and Chinese and Gothic patterns (bottom right) were fashionable although usually only for a particular room rather than a whole house. Paints which had been rather dull previously could now be found in a wider and lighter choice of colours like pea green, Wedgwood blue, soft greys, beige and pinks, while 'stone' colours were still popular. These were now in a matt finish rather than the eggshell sheen which had been used previously and were used to paint all the mouldings including the cornice, although the skirting might be in a dark brown to cover up marks. Pompeii red which was discovered in the remains of this ancient Roman city was also popular in this period although recent studies have shown that it did not exist, but was actually a yellow which had turned to red due to the heat from the volcanic eruption!*

FIG 4.12: Furniture: *A mahogany tripod table (left), a new design of Thomas Chippendale's which became popular in this period and a side table with distinctive elegant tapering legs (right). In this later stage of Chippendale's work the Chinese style was fashionable, distinguished by open fretwork and pagoda-shaped features, while the French style came to the fore after the end of the Seven Year War with France in 1763. As Chippendale's career came to a close, so influence in design came partly from the Adam brothers but more directly from the pattern books of leading designers like Hepplewhite and, later, Thomas Sheraton. Mahogany was still the most popular wood in fashionable houses although different sources meant it was lighter than before and could now have figured curl veneered fronts to the finest pieces. From the 1770s plain carved pieces began losing out to a revival of inlaid decorative work using a lighter satinwood (above right) and then, in the late 1780s, furniture with painted decoration became fashionable for a while. Mahogany could now be found in the bedroom and, despite the habit of moving older pieces up to these rooms, new commodes, washstands and small dressing room items were much in demand from leading cabinet makers.*

FIG 4.13: Adams furniture: *Although the Adam brothers did not directly produce furniture they were very influential in its design, with Hepplewhite and Sheraton both taking elements of their work into their own more affordable pieces. They used the Greek vase or lyre shape in their chair backs, delicately round or square legs, spade feet, honeysuckle and husks, a round or oval feature (based upon Greek paterae (decorated drinking dishes which looked like plates), and fluting (concave grooves). The backs of their chairs could also be upholstered with round, oval and shield shapes and they were also key in making the painting of furniture fashionable (in fact, you would be hard pushed to find any bare wood in some of their interior schemes). Robert Adam died in 1792 and his brother James in 1794 although their influence lasted for many years to come.*

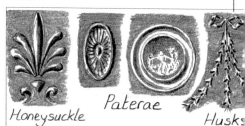

Honeysuckle Paterae Husks

FIG 4.14: Sofas: *In the Tudor or Stuart home there was little in the way of comfort; the only option to benches and stools were settles, straight-backed narrow seats for two or more people. In the late 17th century these developed into upholstered settees or long seats. A version which was popular in the Georgian period was the chair-back settee which literally had two or more wooden chair-backs behind a long upholstered seat. A sofa (probably from the Arabic 'suffah' which means a long upholstered seat) first appeared in the early 1700s and was a larger version of a fully upholstered settee as in this example from the late 18th century.*

FIG 4.16: Country furniture: *Vernacular designs in oak were now being replaced in rural areas by copies of fashionable designs, usually with just the back in the latest urban style as with this late 18th-century, ladder-back type, popular in the north of the country.*

FIG 4.15: Hepplewhite furniture: *Little is known about George Hepplewhite before he arrived in London in the 1760s and his period of direct production was cut short by his early death in 1786. His reputation as a leading designer and influence upon other cabinet makers was established by his* Cabinet Maker and Upholsterer's Guide *which was published in 1788–9 by his widow who also continued the Hepplewhite name in a successful furniture business afterwards. Hepplewhite chairs were distinguished by shield-shaped backs often incorporating the Prince of Wales' plume of feathers as in this example (although he also used oval, heart-shaped and wheel backs which were raised above the seat on uprights). He often incorporated half-wheel decoration at the bottom of the back, liked to use curved elements and fitted tapered straight legs.*

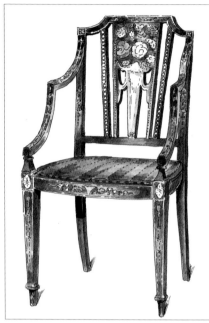

FIG 4.17: Sheraton furniture: *Born in around 1750, Sheraton was a Baptist preacher in his youth and his furniture designs, after he established himself in London during the 1780s, have a puritanical simplicity about them. He preferred straight lines to curves, with straight chair backs, top rails, legs (with thimble feet) and uprights at the base of the arms. He usually had a horizontal bar at the base of the back design which had a notable gap above the seat. Despite this seemingly restricted form, his furniture was graceful and decorative, with ample use of satinwood inlays and painted finishes. He was keen to promote this latter idea which could be applied to a hard wood (as in this example) or a softwood like beech or birch which could be covered with a white or green varnish paint and the background picked out in a strong colour or in gold. His designs also spread with the publication* of his Cabinet Maker and Upholsterer's Drawing Book *(1791–4) and after his death in 1806 he remained influential into the Regency period.*

FIG 4.18: Lighting: *It is hard to imagine in the modern house just how poor lighting was in the past. Up to this period most had to manage with a dim glow from candles or rush lights (literally, rushes or grasses dipped in animal fat) which were dirty, smelly and burnt out quickly, while beeswax candles were only for the well-off. To improve the situation, wall-mounted sconces were fitted with mirrors behind them to try and reflect more light. These matched candelabras or chandeliers which had the candles grouped together for more light. Pewter, glass, and silver or porcelain slender candlesticks were popular in the 1750s and '60s, fluted Corinthian columns in the 1770s, and thicker iron and burnished metal sticks by the 1790s. The main alternative had been oil lamps but these were generally unreliable and dirty so new types introduced in* the 1780s were a vast improvement. They were designed to permit more air to flow around the wick and had the chamber containing the rape seed, olive or palm oil raised above the light so that gravity would improve the flow to the flame, as in this example from the turn of the 19th century.

Chapter ⑤

Regency Styles

1800–1840

FIG 5.1: Family room: *A private room on the ground floor of a large terrace used by the family for leisure, light meals, writing and reading; decorated with distinctive Regency stripes, fluted fireplace surround and an informal arrangement of furniture.*

Although George VI was only Prince Regent from 1811–1820 there are distinct fashions which fit into a broader time-scale in terms of architectural style and interior design such that the Regency period tends to cover the years from 1800 to the 1830s and, in some places, later still. Despite these decades being associated with frivolity and decadence, mainly due to how the Prince himself was viewed at the time, society was in fact facing momentous threats from first Napoleon and then from the aftermath of the war with France. Fear that revolution would spread to these shores, heightened by thousands of soldiers returning to find no work, encouraged the upper classes to present a more dignified and benevolent image and eventually forced the authorities to spread power to a larger section of the population, thus creating a new more influential middle class.

One of the effects of the Napoleonic Wars was an abrupt halt to the Grand Tours of Europe. Instead, young aristocrats turned their attention to home-grown landscapes and ruined medieval structures, or the more distant cultures that they came into contact with through trade with the fledgling empire. Some, inspired by patriotic pride, built mansions in the form of mighty castles, new villages filled with rusticated houses in the Cottage Orne or Tudor style, and a few, whimsical buildings which reflected a taste for the Far East and Ancient Egypt. These styles contrasted with the conventional Classically-inspired houses which, with a coating of stucco (a smooth render), scoured and painted to look like stone, dominated the new estates which were rapidly erected around London, new spa towns like Cheltenham and Leamington and seaside resorts, most notably Brighton.

The detached house and new semi-detached villas which first appeared in this period were arranged in a more familiar layout, with a dining room and drawing room often either side of an entrance hall, and bedrooms on the floor above. Larger terraces were now raised up a few feet so the door was approached up steps and a half basement created below which allowed more light and air into the service rooms. There was a fashion for letting the outside in, with full-height sash windows and, later, French windows at either end of the piano nobile and carefully placed mirrors

reflecting foliage and light, while shallow bow-shaped bay windows allowed those inside to view fashionable passers-by.

Inside, the rooms had gradually become taller, around a foot or so higher than they had been in the early Georgian period. Furnishings and fittings could be found in refined forms or exuberant shapes, although there was a tendency towards straight lines rather than curves. Despite the war, French Empire style was hugely influential inside the home, with the Classical palette boosted at the turn of the 19th century by the publication of Henry Holland's *Etchings*

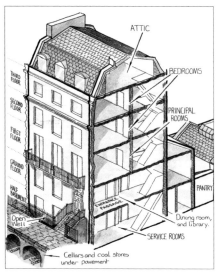

FIG 5.2: *A cut-away view of a large Regency terrace, with a half basement allowing more light into the underground rooms. A growing number of specialist service rooms means that, in this example, the kitchen is a free-standing structure in the yard behind the pantry. Note also the balcony and French windows on the first floor.*

of *Ancient Ornamental Architecture* and discoveries made by Napoleon in Ancient Egypt. Added to this wide variety of sources were new, more vibrant colour schemes, striped wallpapers and fabrics, and a continued acceptance of sham materials, with most interiors covered with painted, stained or grained surfaces and only the finest made from the genuine article.

FIG 5.3: Bedrooms: *A large Regency bedroom with a four-poster, featuring thin, fluted posts and a wardrobe with drawers rather than full-height hanging space. White bed linen was common by this period, and yellows and blues were often recommended as wall colours to offset it. If there was not a separate dressing room to one side, then a washstand would have been in the bedroom, a tall wooden unit with lift-up flaps on top, covering the bowl.*

FIG 5.4: Drawing room: *By this period it was customary for men to stay behind in the dining room after a meal, with the ladies retiring to the more distinctly feminine drawing room which, now that the ladies wore less cumbersome formal wear, could have a more casual and flexible arrangement of furniture (dado rails were still fitted as a result). Richly-upholstered chairs, settees, sofas and chaise longues, with low sofa tables featuring lift-up flaps at each end and Venetian carpets with stripes were all popular.*

FIG 5.5: **Walls:** *Wallpaper grew in popularity, as in these examples, with those which simulated a fabric or decorative effect like flocks and moires (chintzy wood grain effect) and bold stripes being distinctive. Decorative paint effects and gilding were used on walls of stronger colours, with maroon and orangey reds popular in dining rooms, and greens in libraries and drawing rooms. Royal blues and sulphur yellows were also used. Wall mouldings could be painted the same colour as the wall or picked out in white with details in gilt. Coordinating colours were used so carpets, curtains and upholstery were harmonised with the wall colour rather than a scattering of individual pieces and patterns which had been acceptable before.*

FIG 5.6: **Stairs:** *Plain, thin, square balusters with dark wood handrails ending in swirls at the bottom step (right) were very distinctive of Regency stairs. Some had more decorative metalwork (left) and skylights in the roof above.*

FIG 5.7: **Doors:** *A Regency six-panelled door, with labels of parts. The fluted architrave and bulls eyes in the top corners are very distinctive of Regency doorcases and fireplaces. Oval and round metal knobs with brass finger-plates above were popular; surface mounted locks and, later in the period, mortise types set within the door were common as people sought privacy.*

FIG 5.8: Fireplace surrounds: *Marble, hardwood and painted softwood fireplace surrounds in Classical styles (left) and with bulls eyes in the corners (right) were common.*

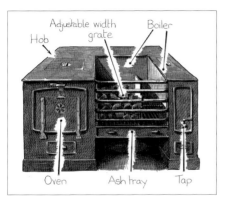

FIG 5.9: Ranges: *Cast-iron kitchen ranges were first developed in the 18th century, with an oven fitted to the side of an adjustable grate with a boiler on the other side first appearing in the 1780s. By the Regency period the boiler was extended round the back of the grate so the heat was always applied even when the grate was reduced in width as in this example. These basic open ranges could be found in areas near coal fields and larger towns and cities.*

FIG 5.10: Grates: *Cast-iron register grates with an adjustable flap over the chimney opening became common during this period (left and centre). In 1797 Count Rumford devised methods which would improve the performance of coal fires, including lowering the basket, narrowing the chimney opening, bringing the fire forward and splaying the sides to reflect more heat into the room. However, only the latter two improvements were generally heeded. Hob grates remained popular, as seen in the example on the right.*

FIG 5.11 : Furniture: *Although there is great variety in Regency furniture, especially by the 1830s, there was a move to less ornate and plain surfaces (compared with 18th-century pieces), with straight, elegant lines replacing the curves and swirls of Hepplewhite in the opening decades of the period. Despite this, the leg which gently curved forward like a sabre (Fig 5.12 and 5.13) and bow-fronted pieces (right) were popular forms. The French Empire style was also a distinctive influence on English designers despite war with Napoleon; its extravagant, strong, and colourful pieces based upon discoveries in Pompeii, Greece and Egypt were adapted here to create an English Empire style. Accurate Classical forms and decoration were now widely used after the publication in 1799–1800 of the architect Henry Holland's* Etchings of Ancient Ornamental Architecture *and Thomas Hope's 1807 book* Household Furniture and Decoration, *in which he created adaptations of actual pieces of ancient furniture complete with winged beasts, lyres and Egyptian heads (the fashion for Egyptian decorative style was popular mainly in the first decade of the century). The drawings and designs were watered down for a more general middle class public by, at first, Sheraton in his 1803 Directory and the 1804–6 The Cabinet Maker and Artist's Encyclopaedia and then by George Smith in his 1808 publication* A Collection of Designs for Household Furniture and Interior Decoration. *The Chinese style was still fashionable with black and gold lacquered finishes popular, as well as pieces with an Indian or Gothic theme, and it was acceptable for these exotic and domestic sources to be applied to classical forms of furniture. Regency furniture used mahogany for the main structure but rosewood and zebrawood were used for veneering, and brass was often inset to create decorative details (see Fig 5.12).*

FIG 5.12: Sofa table: *Languid relaxation was a theme of the day and sofas with low backs and scrolled ends were seen as a necessity in the finest houses. Alongside this was the Regency innovation of the sofa table, a low piece with flaps at either end and castors shaped like lion's paws on curving legs, so the table could be moved to save the individual having to move.*

FIG 5.13: **Dining tables:** *Regency tables were generally permanent fixtures in the centre of the dining room so clever flaps and sliding section were no longer a necessity although they could still be found. The finest examples had bulky pedestals often standing upon sabre-shaped tripod legs with brass castors as in this example, two on rectangular ones and a single one on round tables. This form was also found on other smaller side tables.*

FIG 5.14: **Mirror:** *Round mirrors with convex glass and gilt plaster work or carved frames featuring balls around their perimeter were distinctive of the Regency period. Naturalistic decoration like vines and water leaf (a simple undulating laurel leaf design) were popular later in the period. Eagles mounting the tops of mirrors and other pieces of furniture were inspired by French Empire designs from around 1800 and then Russian eagles were popular after Napoleon's disastrous retreat from the country in 1808.*

FIG 5.15: **Chiffonier:** *A smaller version of a sideboard which could be found in middle-class homes in this period. It typically had two doors across the front and a raised shelf at the rear of the top edged with pierced brass as in this example. Pleated silk behind glass doors was a distinctive feature of Regency furniture.*

FIG 5.16: Chairs: *Regency chairs were generally lower than earlier types and could be made from mahogany, rosewood or painted softwood as in the English Empire style example (top left). Legs tend to be straight and round with peg-top feet, many with fluted decoration. Some had sabre-shaped legs and gilt or brass Classical details copied from the leading pattern books of the day or naval-inspired decorative motifs like anchors and ropes. The shape of backs changed through the period as broad top rails and horizontal splats were more common than vertical types (top left and bottom right). A distinctive form of chair from this period was the bergère (top right) which had a more relaxed form with upholstered cushions on top of a mahogany frame and caning to the sides and back.*

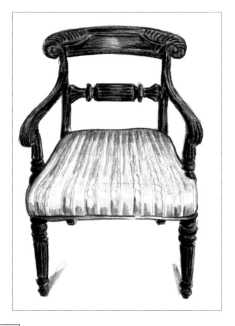

FIG 5.17: Fabrics: *Upholstery and curtain fabrics were now often coordinated with wall coverings and carpets in the most fashionable interior schemes. Stronger colours became popular in a printed pattern with a lighter tint of the same or complementary colour in the background. Furniture was covered in woven or printed fabrics like striped silks (left), damasks (centre) and chintzes (right), and leather was used in libraries and dining rooms. Loose covers were often used to protect chairs from daily use. The same pattern often featured on both curtains and furniture, with the main part of the design centred on the back of chairs. Classical motifs like wreaths, lyres and sphinxes could be found and stripes were very distinctive of the period. Popular colours included deep greens, strong yellows, royal blues and reds, the latter especially in the 1820s and '30s.*

FIG 5.18: Chaise longue: *Regency sofas often featured roll-top ends and carved feet like a Grecian couch, another variant of this being the daybed, a long upholstered*

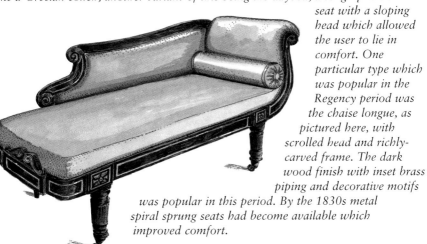

seat with a sloping head which allowed the user to lie in comfort. One particular type which was popular in the Regency period was the chaise longue, as pictured here, with scrolled head and richly-carved frame. The dark wood finish with inset brass piping and decorative motifs was popular in this period. By the 1830s metal spiral sprung seats had become available which improved comfort.

FIG 5.19: Fittings: *Before the late 17th century, furniture had wooden knobs or iron fittings but during the reign of William and Mary brass drop and loop handles with solid plates running the full length of the handle were introduced. In the early 18th century the back was often pierced and, a little later, roses at each end of the drop handle were common. By the turn of the 19th century elaborate versions of these with the latest Classical details could be found (centre) while round back plates with concentric circle patterns (like the bulls eyes on fireplaces and door surrounds) with the handle draped around its edge (left) were distinctive of the Regency period. Lion's head handles (right) came into fashion in the late 18th century and could be found in larger versions on front doors and smaller versions on furniture.*

FIG 5.20: Moulding: *Reeded and fluted mouldings were distinctive of Regency furniture and fittings.*

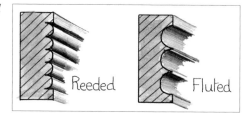

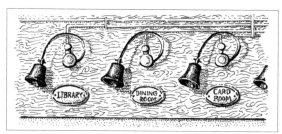

FIG 5.21 Bell boards: *A new feature which could be found in the largest houses were bells by which servants could be summoned. Previously they had to sit in the hall and wait to be called but now these systems with wires running through pipes to cords in each room connected to a board in the servants' hall or a corridor were more convenient for both sides.*

Chapter **6**

Early Victorian Styles

1840–1880

FIG 6.1: Drawing room: *Victorian interiors tend to be imagined as strongly-coloured, busily-patterned and crammed full of furnishings and fittings, a characteristic that is certainly true of drawing rooms in the 1860s and '70s as in the example here. All manner of furniture, ornaments, plants, screens, and the requisite piano were seemingly thrown together to display the owner's wealth and taste.*

This early and mid Victorian period was one of great change within society which is reflected in the dark, colourful and cluttered interiors which characterise the 1860s and '70s. It was a time of fluctuating fortunes for all classes although there was a general rise in wages and conditions towards the end of the period. Thousands of people from the country moved into the towns and cities while the slums which this shift created encouraged the wealthy to move out to new, private estates in the suburbs. The middle classes grew in numbers, influence and ambition and could display their new-found confidence in the home now that mass production brought luxurious furnishings and fittings within their grasp while museums, shops and magazines guided their taste. Their sons could join the ranks of the upper classes in going to university and then, rather than taking a grand tour of Europe, the Victorian gentlemen travelled to colonial outposts or toured the medieval remains and mountainous landscapes within Great Britain, a shift in inspiration which would directly affect the styles of the day and cut the country off from the main flow of Continental fashions.

In the 1840s and '50s a battle of the styles ensued between those who advocated the Classical orders and those who thought a home-grown Gothic style was more appropriate. In the wake of the French Revolution and the Napoleonic Wars, a large quantity of medieval artefacts had come on the market while at the same time the first detailed studies of buildings from the Middle Ages provided sources of information for designers like A.W.N. Pugin who transformed the pointed arch and Gothic motifs into a new art form. Pugin and those he inspired advocated a new honesty in building, rejecting Regency imitation materials. They believed the arrangement of rooms should be freed from strict rules on symmetry and the decoration of surfaces should be two dimensional. At first, interiors reflected the eclectic mix of styles which had been

acceptable in the closing years of the Regency but by the 1860s the Gothic style and Pugin's doctrine were influencing the most fashionable homes. Despite publications like *Hints on Household Taste* by Charles L. Eastlake and the work of William Morris in promoting good interior design, it is likely that most middle-class owners chose busy, mass-produced Gothic and floral papers and combinations of colours with varying success. They probably reflected their love of pattern and richly-decorated surfaces rather than their concern with the quality of design and correct arrangements of furnishings.

FIG 6.2: *Kitchens came out of the basement during this period and could be found at the rear, ranging from spacious examples like this one catering for numerous guests in a large house down to a compact room in a rear extension. In many smaller houses, preparation and cooking was done in the rear living room and washing in a scullery at the back. Kitchens always had free-standing tables and dressers, with a cast-iron range providing hot water and an oven (sometimes with an additional open fire in the largest). Walls were usually part-whitewashed and part-tiled.*

The housing stock was still dominated by the terrace in all manner of sizes, with semis still only accounting for a small percentage and detached villas, now asymmetrically designed, for the wealthiest owner. Privacy was becoming an important consideration for families and throughout this period the house gradually withdraws from public view. Gone were the balconies to watch passers-by, now walls and front gardens kept prying eyes at bay. Service rooms came out of the basement and were sited in larger rear extensions, thus allowing servants to move up and down the backstairs, with minimal contact with family and guests. Most middle-class houses imitated this with short, rear extensions of just one storey at first, becoming two storeys high later in the period, with the upper part either becoming an additional bedroom or a new bathroom (those which were the former were often converted into the latter soon after).

The hallway in which guests could wait before being shown in to see the family was an important feature for privacy-seeking Victorians, with narrow passageways being squeezed into even the smallest middle-class houses. Dining rooms maintained their masculine emphasis with strong coloured patterns and sturdy dark wood or black marble fireplace surrounds, although they tended to be less cluttered than the drawing room which became a depository for all manner of ornaments, books, pictures and plants. In larger houses there were more numerous rooms with specific roles than in the past. In addition to morning or breakfast rooms, there would be a study or library with wood-panelled or leather-effect wall coverings, Gothic or Elizabethan style furniture, and pieces of armour or stuffed animals

FIG 6.3: Hall: *This became an important space for owners where guests could wait before being shown into a reception room. Patterned ceramic-tiled floors were the most distinctive feature of this period and colourful examples became popular from the 1850s. The dado rail protected walls and was covered below with a leather or marble effect, wood panelling, wall tiles from the 1860s, and embossed papers from the late 1870s while, above, a brown, burgundy or dark green patterned wallpaper was popular. This wider example from the late 19th century with its glazed front door also has a cast-iron umbrella stand and compact fireplace and a wooden hall chair and table which were often fitted where space permitted.*

FIG 6.4: Bedrooms: *It was still the custom for couples in larger houses to have separate bedrooms, although they could be linked by a door, with a boudoir for the lady and a dressing room for the gentleman. The middle classes imitated this by having twin beds for husband and wife. A notable change for children in this period was the need to have separate bedrooms for the sexes, a reform which put pressure on the family for additional rooms. Although wooden four-posters could still be found, half-testers with drapery over the head of the bed were more popular with brass bedsteads becoming common by the 1850s although the curtains fell from fashion from the 1860s as they were seen as dirt traps. The main bedroom was now a private family room and the decor and furnishings were plainer and lighter than elsewhere in the house. Walls were papered with simple repeated patterns and florals, or painted in light pinks, blues, and grey, while the cornice might be picked out in a colour to match the fabrics. Curtains were lighter and less fussy than in reception rooms, with cretonne (a heavy printed cotton or linen), chintz, dimity (a cotton with raised woven stripes) and patterned muslin proving popular fabrics.*

which were characteristic of the age, while smoking or billiard rooms were often decorated with a Moorish or Turkish theme reflecting their reputations for masculine impropriety!

FIG 6.5: Bathrooms: *With the necessary improvement in mains water pressure required to supply the upstairs of a house and improved drainage, a purpose-built bathroom in new houses became practical from the 1860s. These early types tended to have the bath tub and basin (known as a lavatory at this time) boxed in panelled wood.*

FIG 6.6: Ceilings: *The ceiling could feature colourful deep moulded patterns to match the style of the room or be plain white, with a ceiling rose above the light to hide the soot marks from the flame.*

In more modest middle-class homes there would usually be a parlour at the front reserved for special occasions, with an everyday living room at the rear and a kitchen or scullery behind this. Bathrooms begin to appear in this class of house from the 1870s although initially they were not popular in the finest houses where the wealthy still had numerous servants to bring hot water up to their bathtubs! Toilets began to be fitted in houses from the

FIG 6.7: Wall decoration: *The fashion for dividing the wall horizontally with moulding fell from favour in the mid 19th century. Skirting boards could be painted brown or grained to look like a finer wood, while cornices were boldly-coloured or complemented the colour of the fabrics in the room. Early on, lighter paints were still used – creams, greys, green, pink, lilac and blue – but, by the 1850s, stronger colours like browns, reds, terracotta, olive green, burgundy and purple become popular, with slightly more muted colours like sage green and rose later in this period. Leading designers like Pugin and Morris advocated wallpaper with simple two-dimensional patterns and repeating motifs (top row). However, it is likely that the poorly-designed brash florals, imitation marble, and papers featuring scenes like famous battles (bottom row) remained popular with the masses. Flowers, plants, animals and trellis work could still be found early in this period, with Gothic-inspired designs coming to prominence later on. Dark red and green flock papers were used in dining rooms, while plum, greens, gold, rose and strong blues were used on drawing room papers.*

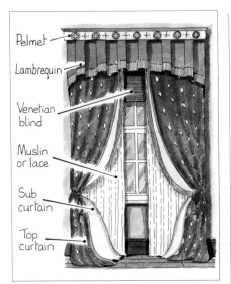

Pelmet
Lambrequin
Venetian blind
Muslin or lace
Sub curtain
Top curtain

FIG 6.8: Curtains: *In the main reception rooms the curtains in this period could be as many as four layers thick, not just for show but to act as a barrier against dirt and sunlight which could damage furnishings. First there would have been a Venetian or roller blind up against the window, the latter becoming common by the mid century with a plain white or patterned finish and, in some cases, a painted scene across it. The next layer inwards would have been a sub curtain of lace or muslin which could have been drawn across to collect dirt but still let light in when the window was open. There could then be a set of curtains in chintz, damask, or a heavier fabric like cretonne (usually in a floral design) or velvet within the finest rooms, and a fourth layer comprising a brocatelle (a heavy embossed cotton appearing like a damask) or a tapestry. The curtains would be hung off a wooden or brass pole in most Gothic Revival houses and gathered up at the sides on hooks and allowed to spread out over the floor at the bottom.*

1860s as sewerage improved. At first, earth closets in which soil, sawdust or ash was dropped into a bucket were popular, fitted into a cupboard or under the stairs, but by the 1870s water closets in a small room upstairs or in a lean-to at the rear were appearing.

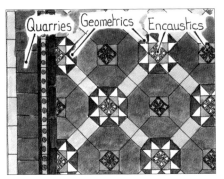

Quarries   Geometrics   Encaustics

FIG 6.9: Ceramic floor tiles: *The most distinctive feature of mid and late Victorian houses is their patterned ceramic-tiled floors in the hallway and sometimes in the living room. They were made up from plains (quarries) with geometric-shaped tiles in cream, red, brown and black (and later green and blue) forming the patterns. Within this there would usually be some encaustic tiles. These were based on medieval types with a design stamped in the wet clay and a different coloured slip (a watery clay with a pigment) poured into it before firing. The finished floor was usually unglazed and was polished afterwards with linseed oil or wax. In service rooms plain reds and blacks were usually used. From the 1860s, mass-produced glazed wall tiles with fashionable patterns were being used below the dado in halls and around fireplaces, some with a raised edge to the design and a coloured glaze within.*

FIG 6.10: Wall mouldings: *Although a dado rail and picture rail were optional, a skirting board at the bottom of the wall was a permanent fixture; Victorian types being notably higher than before, usually with a simple rounded top. Cornices tend to be more elaborate than Regency types and during the second half of the century can be found spreading out horizontally across the ceiling.*

FIG 6.11: Floors: *The inventive Victorians began producing a wide range of floor coverings in addition to traditional types like Oriental rugs which remained desirable in the finest homes. For a while, in the mid century, fully-fitted carpets were once again in fashion before the problem of cleaning them made smaller movable pieces with painted boards or parquet around the edge the preferred choice (usually a gap of around 3 ft). Mass production of carpets was slow to develop due to the high cost of machinery but by the 1860s cheaper versions were widely available. Wilton (with a cut loop producing a velvet pile), Kidderminster (with a reversible flat weave) and Axminster (with a knotted pile) were still the most desirable and a luxury item reserved for principal rooms where they spent most of the time covered up by cheaper materials for protection. Designs ranged from simple patterns and stripes in the 1840s, to Gothic-style fleur-de-lys, tracery, quatrefoils and heraldic motifs, Rococo styles, florals and even tartan. Floor cloths used as a cheaper permanent covering or to protect carpets were large pieces of canvas which were stitched together and then covered in layers of size and paint with a final pattern applied (which often imitated other floorings) before being left to season for up to six months. Linoleum was introduced in the late 1860s, a mix of tiny pieces of cork and wood bound together in linseed oil, resins and wax which was pressed onto a canvas backing producing a flat and hygienic surface, ideal for nurseries and bedrooms. The boards beneath these coverings were now machine cut with regular sized planks (wide at first but becoming thinner towards the end of the century) and straight edges often held together with a separate dowel or tongue and then painted or grained to appear like a hardwood.*

FIG 6.12: Fabric designs: *Woven fabrics with highlighted floral patterns (right), simple geometric patterns, damasks (left), heraldic designs and Gothic motifs (centre) were popular in the early Victorian period. With the introduction of aniline dyes in the 1850s printed fabrics began to be produced with stronger and more consistent colours with designs often inspired by Owen Jones's books. These boldly-patterned fabrics were used for both curtaining and upholstery, with plain velvets and rep (a ribbed cotton or wool) popular on the latter, while both were frequently finished with tassels.*

FIG 6.13: Fireplace surrounds: *Marble fireplace surrounds in white or grey in the drawing room and black with coloured veins in the dining room were desirable. Early on, they were usually fairly plain in design, typically with a couple of scrolls or foliage supporting an increasingly deep mantel shelf (top centre). Hardwood and carved stone designs were popular, especially in Gothic interiors (top left), and all finishes were imitated on cheaper softwood surrounds. Slate and cast-iron also became popular; the latter for sometimes complicated designs and for simple surrounds in bedrooms and service rooms (bottom right).*

Smoke curtains or pelmets draped down from the mantel (top right) were popular from the 1860s while small screens were often placed in front of the fire to protect delicate furnishings.

FIG 6.14 : Grates: *The concave, arched grate pictured here is distinctive of the 1850s and '60s and was designed to reflect more heat back into the room. The hinged register at the rear, covering the chimney opening (which was now reduced to under 10 inches) and a corrugated firebrick to allow more air up the back also helped improve the performance of coal fires.*

FIG 6.15: Door knobs: *Four-panelled doors had replaced six-panelled ones by the mid 19th century and, in general, the mouldings became deeper. Brass, china and wooden knobs were usually fitted with finger plates in the same material.*

Risers

Balustrade

Open string: with balustrade resting on treads.

Treads

Newel post

String

Panelling

Closed String: balustrade rests on side string.

FIG 6.16: Stairs: *The Victorian obsession with revival is clearly evident in the joinery within the house, especially the staircase where the simple, elegant, open string and thin balusters of the Regency era which could still be found early in this period were superseded by a return to closed string staircases with newel posts. In general, furnishings and fittings from the 1840s to 1880s have been dismissed by 20th-century art critics because of this and the dominance of mass-produced elements which, in the case of staircases, meant turned wooden parts became cheaper and an elaborate balustrade could extend further up the house and not just the part in view of guests. Brass rods holding thin strips of carpet down the steps and frog profile handrails were popular in this period.*

FIG 6.17: Dining room furniture: *As with stairs, the graceful designs of the previous period are replaced by copies of 17th-and 18th-century pieces, much of which was mass produced and rather bulky and curvaceous. In the dining room, richly-carved furniture included hardwood tables, now usually with a rectangular top with small curved corners (as in this example) or had complete semi-circular ends and bulbous Jacobean or more elegant 18th-century types of leg. Another distinctive feature was the sideboard which now typically had a back, with cupboards or shelves flanking a central mirror on which the finest silver, china and glass could be displayed.*

FIG 6.18: Chairs and sofas: *One advantage of Victorian seating over past designs is that it was more comfortable now that coiled strings and buttoned upholstery became popular from the 1850s. This was indeed fortunate as meals could have more than six courses! Dining chairs with balloon-shaped curving backs and a leather or tapestry seat (centre) were distinctive of the period and similar forms were often used on upholstered armchairs (left), while sofas which looked like two chairs linked (compact versions are often referred to as love chairs) were also popular (right). There was also a vast array of styles and types available from compact mahogany chairs for the hall to deeply-stuffed leather Chesterfield sofas.*

FIG 6.19: Bedroom furniture: *From the middle of the 19th century, manufacturers began producing complete suites of furniture for the bedroom. Mahogany, rosewood, and walnut were used, with lighter woods coming on the market from the 1870s. Wardrobes like this example still tended to have shelves inside for clothes rather than hanging space, while washstands ranged from bow-fronted pieces with a basin set within the top to later square types with a slab of marble or wooden top with a low tiled splash back.*

FIG 6.20: Lighting: *Although gas lighting had been introduced into some homes in the previous period, it had mainly been supplied to industry, and it was not until its installation into the new Houses of Parliament in the 1850s that demand grew for it in the home. These early gas lights had their fish-tale or batwing-shaped burner pointing upwards and were much brighter than oil lamps (but less than*

half as bright as modern bulbs). Unfortunately they gave off gases and soot so tended to only be used downstairs with ceiling roses above them to collect the dirt (in some cases these had holes allowing the fumes to pass through and be drawn out through ducts hidden under the floorboards). There were also improvements made to oil lamps with the introduction of paraffin in the 1850s which meant the reservoir could now be below the burner as it was thinner and didn't need gravity to draw it up. Shades on these light sources could be as ornate as other interior features with flower-shaped clear or coloured glass and silk, linen and parchment types often finished off with tassels or beads. A wax hardening process, the use of paraffin wax and mass production made candles which burned longer and evenly available to the majority of the population. Candlesticks and holders could be found made from bronze, glass, brass, ceramics, iron and silver or an imitation of it.

Chapter 7

Late Victorian and Edwardian Styles

1880–1920

FIG 7.1: The Hall, Blackwell Arts and Crafts House, Windermere: *Interiors of large houses now took on a more homely scale, inspired by 17th-century manors and farmhouses rather than castles and churches. The control of space and light was mastered by leading Arts and Crafts architects as in this example by M.H. Baillie Scott and although the sources were historic, the structure and approach were modern, and gradually the architects' belief in simple and honest design began to filter down to the middle classes.*

This period, in which many of the foundations of the modern world were at least theorised over if not put into practice, was shattered by the First World War. During these late Victorian and Edwardian years there was much unrest and concern about the state of the nation. Competition from abroad, modern inventions and the breakdown of the old aristocratic order only intensified the public's rather insular attitude. The glorification of our medieval past and expanding empire masked these problems whilst the Continental style was looked upon as strange and alien. Middle-class anxieties were relieved somewhat by the Arts and Craft movement. Principally, this was a social movement inspired by the writings of John Ruskin and the work of William Morris. The movement sought to return dignity to workers overwhelmed by factory production. This would be achieved by training and creating opportunities for craftsmen who could design, make and market their own furnishings and fittings. Although their use of local materials and rejection of the machine ultimately made the goods produced under this broad banner too expensive and rather elitist, they did raise the standard of design and set in place ideals which would inspire the next generation of architects.

Despite a revival of Classical buildings in the Edwardian period, the vast majority of speculative-built, detached, semi and terraced housing reflected the fashion for our domestic past with mock timber-framing, hanging tiles, and casement windows covering the façade. The Aesthetic movement of the 1870s introduced new ideas of beauty and simplicity into interior design, while architects like Norman Shaw, Voysey and Baillee Scott reinterpreted the past and responded to the needs of the owner, controlling light and space to create inventive new living halls (see Fig 7.1) and bright drawing rooms. Although

these new interiors were too daring for most tastes, some of their ideas filtered down to middle-class housing. Simplified two-dimensional designs on wallpapers, fabrics and tiles, lighter colours and a more restrained use of ornamentation meant that despite still appearing cluttered to modern eyes they were less oppressive than earlier Victorian rooms.

The majority of this new housing was

FIG 7.2: Hall: *The entrance into the late Victorian and Edwardian house could range from a narrow passage in a terrace to a complete room in larger Arts and Crafts houses. The decor in most still reflected the need to hide dirt and everyday knocks so was still dark to modern eyes, with the walls protected with a dado rail and an anaglypta paper below and a light pattern or plain paint above. Popular colours included blues, terracotta and greens, with browns and gold for the lower section. Black and white ceramic tiled floors were very popular in Edwardian houses.*

in rapidly expanding suburbs where cheaper land meant the structure could be larger. In some cases local architects and builders created detached properties along the lines of the leading Arts and Crafts architects with an asymmetrical plan and the entrance leading into a square room which imitated a medieval hall and a kitchen built into the structure of the house. With the extra space in suburban terraces, a hallway was a welcome addition for many families moving out of narrow urban properties while, in larger houses, the passageway was wider with glazed doors and flanking windows and room for compact furniture and a fireplace (see Fig 6.3). Bathrooms were now common in middle-class homes, with a separate water closet alongside.

FIG 7.3: Drawing room: *This remained a feminine room, with lighter floral and patterned papers often with a frieze above the picture rail which became fashionable during this period. Colours like rose pink, cream, light greens and lavender, stencilled designs and patterned plaster or embossed paper ceilings were all popular in this room. The fireplace often featured an overmantel above it with shelving for ornaments and, in the finest examples, glass-fronted cupboards either side; these usually being painted white, a relatively rare choice before this period. The interior was further lightened by French doors which now that drains had been improved made the garden a welcome place to be.*

FIG 7.4: Dining room: *Strong colours like red, green and blue remained popular and patterned or striped papers were used. These provided a good background for paintings which were now hung from a picture rail. (Note: In Edwardian houses it was common for the rail to line up with the top of the door.) The fireplace surround was usually in a dark wood, slate or marble with tiled cheeks and, in some houses, the walls were panelled, with Arts and Crafts designers advocating lighter, unstained timbers like oak.*

FIG 7.5: Bathrooms: *It was only in this period that the bathroom became a common fitting in middle-class homes. Many of the upper classes were still reluctant to accept it while they had servants and it would not be until after the Second World War that it was standard in cheaper housing. Unlike the earliest examples, concerns with sanitation meant that most fittings were now not boxed in and even pipes were left exposed, with the sides of the bath sometimes decorated to add a bit of colour. Enamelled metal roll-top baths were introduced from the 1880s standing on ball or claw feet and a matching ceramic wash basin (still referred to as a lavatory in this period) with nickel or brass cross head taps. The toilet or water closet was usually in a separate room; high-level cisterns were usually fitted although low-level types were available from the late 1890s, and the ceramic bowl was sometimes painted inside and out with flowers or landscapes.*

FIG 7.6: Bedrooms: *The general theme of lightening the interior continued in the bedroom with pale pinks, beige, blues and peach on the walls, cream or light greens on the joinery and white for the ceiling. Patterned wallpapers featuring fruits, flowers and ribbons, and chintz curtains in pale tones were popular, and papers specifically designed for nurseries became available. Built-in furniture appeared in some fashionable bedrooms, with white-painted cupboards and shelving either side of the fireplace or a wash stand with fittings above. As two-storey, bay windows were now common on larger middle-class houses so the dresser could be sited within this much lighter space.*

FIG 7.7: Kitchens: *In larger Edwardian houses the kitchen could now be sited within the main body of the house; some with built-in furniture, as in this example. In most cases the sink was still used for cooking, with a separate washroom or scullery provided for laundry.*

FIG 7.8: Closed ranges: *The closed range in which the fire was encased between the ovens was the centrepiece of most kitchens. The boiler was now usually sited at the rear, with hotplates on the upper surface. The front of the fire could be exposed and a roaster with a rotating spit sited in front of it. The ranges needed a lot of maintenance and gas cookers gained in popularity.*

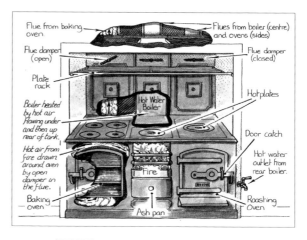

FIG 7.9: Walls: *Two-dimensional patterns advocated by leading designers like William Morris and C.F.A. Voysey (top and bottom left) began influencing wallpaper design (top centre and right) although shadowing and highlights still appeared on many papers. Matching designs were produced for the frieze above the picture rail, or an embossed paper or stencilling with a pattern to complement the use of the room (i.e. fruit in the dining room). Later in this period colours became lighter and fashionable interiors began to use paints rather than wallpaper, with bright whites introduced in the 1890s for the joinery.*

FIG 7.10: Wall tiles: *Glazed wall tiles became more affordable and fashionable throughout the house, being used in the kitchens, bathroom, hall and around the doorway on the outside. Some of the finest, though, could be found on the cheeks of cast-iron register grates, angled to reflect more heat back into the room. These could be in traditional patterns, blue and white Delft types (popularised by Arts and Crafts architects) or in Art Nouveau stylised floral designs as in the example above.*

FIG 7.11: Anaglypta: *Embossed papers like Anaglypta were very fashionable, especially in halls. These two examples, with stylised floral patterns in an Art Nouveau style, were one of the few times that this continental taste could be found in the English home.*

FIG 7.12: **Fireplace surrounds:** *Overmantels and built-in shelving and cupboards were a distinctive feature of Edwardian fireplace surrounds. Leading designers like Charles Rennie Mackintosh created stark, almost modern, pieces (bottom left), although these were too daring for most tastes.*

FIG 7.13: **Register grates:** *The register grate was improved upon in this period, with adjustable vents fitted in the ash pan to control the rate of combustion, tiled splays to reflect the heat back in and the fire brought forward with a hood above to draw the smoke back up the chimney (with beaten copper ones popular in Arts and Crafts interiors). Wood burning grates in inglenooks were reintroduced in some large houses.*

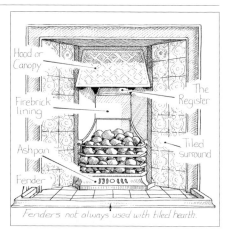

FIG 7.14: Doors: *Four-panelled internal doors were still dominant but by the turn of the century there was a greater variety available to suit the wide range of styles. Glazed uppers (usually frosted, etched or filled with coloured glass) were popular for front doors and, in some houses, for the partitions between the front and rear reception rooms.*

FIG 7.15: Door furniture: *Knobs were still usually fitted to internal doors, some handles like the hand-made iron example (bottom right) were fitted in Arts and Crafts interiors. Brass, wood, glass and ceramic was widely used for fittings, the beehive shape (top centre) being particularly popular. Finger plates in matching materials or with a design beaten out of copper, (as in the example bottom left), were usually fitted above the knob.*

FIG 7.16: Fabrics: *Designs could vary from two-dimensional, stylised natural forms created by Arts and Crafts designers (left) to more widely-used, elaborate floral patterns (right) which although still busy were simpler and lighter than those in the previous period.*

FIG 7.17: Curtains: *Curtains were simplified over previous multi-layered arrangements, with typically one main set (a heavier pair for winter and a lighter pair for summer), with blinds or nets behind (nets were often only on the lower half of sash windows as pictured here). Lightweight cottons and linens, cretonne (a ribbed effect cotton) and chintz were in fashion although concerns with hygiene meant that the latter could lose its sheen when washed. Pelmets were still fitted, though with less fussy designs like a simple pleat, while many Arts and Crafts interiors only had metal or wooden rails with no lavish trimmings.*

FIG 7.18: Floors: *Most floors were still timber planks which were stained or painted and covered by a large rug or carpet piece (fitted carpets had fallen from favour due to difficulty in cleaning). Parquet flooring was popular (see left) and linoleum in kitchens, bedrooms and nurseries.*

FIG 7.19: Furniture: *Although the obsession with imitating old styles of furniture still dominated the mass market in this period, Arts and Crafts designers were creating beautiful, graceful and inventive pieces, made by skilled craftsmen such as this cabinet by C.F.A. Voysey.*

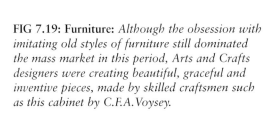

FIG 7.20: Furniture: *The woods used were generally lighter than before; teak and chestnut, in addition to mahogany and oak, were the most popular. Arts and Crafts furniture was rather exclusive as it was generally hand-made, with oak, yew and elm, and pewter, iron or brass fittings. It could be rustic, solid and plain as in this dresser (left) or delicate, elegant and finely-detailed, in general with a plain, functional structure and decoration limited to intricate metalwork. However, it was not cheap and many guilds failed as they could not compete with mass-produced copies produced for shops like Heals and Liberty's. Reproduction furniture was popular, especially Georgian Chippendale, Hepplewhite and Sheraton pieces, while wicker and bamboo pieces were used in drawing rooms and verandahs.*

FIG 7.21: Chairs: *Traditional cottage-style chairs were reinvented by Arts and Crafts designers (left) often using simple oak frames and rush work seats while reinterpretations of Georgian dining room chairs (right) were popular. In general, chairs had more upright backs, with armchairs and sofas often having loose covers. Upholstery included floral chintzes, silks and leather.*

FIG 7.22: Ornaments: *Prominent stylised natural forms like the distinctive trunk and stained glass leaves of this Tiffany lamp (above) and mixed with Celtic forms in this piece by Archibald Knox (below) were distinctive Art Nouveau-inspired pieces from the first decade of the 20th century.*

FIG 7.23: Gas lights: *By the 1890s gas lights had been improved upon, with new incandescent burners and the light turned to point down to reduce shadows (top). A single pendant light in the centre of the room, perhaps with wall sconces either side of the fireplace, and decorative lanterns in the hall (bottom) were common. Electricity started to be fitted into new houses although it was not universal even by the First World War. The design of bulb was constantly adapted to improve performance, yet with only a couple of sockets in the house there was limited opportunity for electric lamps to be used. It is likely that many older houses still had no gas or electric lighting by the end of this period.*

Chapter 8

Inter and Post War Styles

1920–1960

FIG 8.1: *A 1930s living room (left) and one from the late 1950s (right) showing the dramatic transformation that was possible during this period. The earlier example is already lighter and less cluttered than its Victorian forebears but the later setting has an even lower ceiling, functional fittings, plain and bright decoration, with a television replacing the piano.*

This final period seems to be characterised by stark contrasts in society, from the opulence of Hollywood movies and Agatha Christie books to the suffering of the Great Depression and the Jarrow March. The two world wars caused personal loss on a scale not witnessed before but, at the same time, created a desire for change and an acceptance of modernity. The actions taken by governments in the previous period began to unlock the huge wealth held in aristocratic hands and spread it more evenly through society, with a booming middle class benefiting from cheaper mortgages and those of the working class with a steady job from new council estates.

The vast majority of new housing was now in suburban estates as large-scale building companies dug up great swathes of cheap agricultural land and erected avenues, crescents and cul-de-sacs lined with semis. These distinctive forms of housing, with a hipped roof and large bay windows had the front door positioned to the outside of the pair leading into a more spacious hall. After the Second World War this generous size of building plot was gradually reduced as a chronic demand for new housing and limited funds forced builders to squeeze more houses onto each acre.

Although the Arts and Crafts style still influenced the appearance of houses in the 1920s and '30s, the next generation of designers sought to integrate the machine into the production of furnishings, using modern geometric forms with exotic and Egyptian sources to create a new Global style, today referred to as Art Deco. Although bright, streamlined buildings and stepped glass and chrome fittings seem to characterise this period, it was more distinctive of industrial buildings and cinemas. Most owners stuck with the odd traditional-styled pieces intermingled with hand-me-downs. By the mid 1950s a more general acceptance of modernism, coupled with new materials and mass production, made this style of furniture and decoration affordable.

The wider plot for new suburban houses meant a more spacious interior with typically a separate front living room and rear dining room leading off a hallway with a prominent staircase and balustrade. The kitchen tucked in the rear corner now had the washing and cooking facilities combined in one space, with freestanding fittings and a larder cupboard usually under the stairs (now often knocked out). Picture rails were still common in inter war houses but plain walls with just a skirting have been standard ever since. The most modern and optimistic houses in the 1930s celebrated the sun not only with large expanses of metal-framed windows but with the addition of a balcony or sun lounge on a flat roof. This is the period when gardening spread to the masses and the rear of middle-class houses was opened up with bay windows and French doors making the garden a part of the home.

FIG 8.2: 1930s hall: *With cheaper land in the suburbs, the width of the house could be greater and much of this was spent making a grand entrance. Rather than the narrow corridor of the late Victorian terrace, owners could benefit from a spacious hall with a prominent stairs brought forward with room for a balustrade, and room for small pieces of furniture. A window to the side of the door made this a lighter space with geometric patterns replacing earlier floral and heraldic designs.*

FIG 8.3: 1930s living room: *Many living rooms in this period would have been a mix of old and new as in this example: an Art Deco radio, sideboard, armchair and fireplace, alongside hand-me-down pieces of furniture, a rug on the floorboards and a piano.*

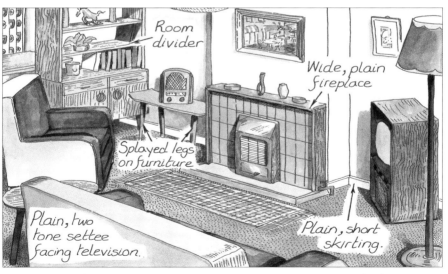

FIG 8.4: 1950s living room: *To save room in many 1950s properties, the dining room and living room were combined into one space, with a room divider to separate off the eating area. Furnishings are brighter and simplified, gas or electric fires have replaced the coal grate and the new television is becoming the focus of the room.*

FIG 8.5: 1930s dining room: *The better-off could fit their living room out with the latest Art Deco furnishings as in this example, with a sideboard, drinks cabinet, rug and a stepped outline to the fireplace, mirror, pelmet and lights. Note the serving hatch leading to the kitchen, a popular feature from the 1930s into the 1970s.*

Freestanding gas or electric cooker.

Instantaneous water heater.

Freestanding gas or electric refrigerator.

Washing machine with built in wringer and vertical cylinder.

Solid fuel hot water boiler.

FIG 8.6: 1950s kitchen: *From the 1920s the kitchen was usually built into the main structure of the house but in spite of contemporary adverts displaying the virtues of built-in furniture, most people, even in the 1950s, would have had only a few fitted pieces. Range cookers had been replaced by a solid fuel water boiler and a separate gas or electric cooker, a washing machine reduced the chore of wash day, and a refrigerator was becoming popular. Freezers were rare as most people still shopped daily.*

FIG 8.7: Wallpapers: *The more daring interiors in the 1920s and '30s could use bold geometric Art Deco patterns (far left) or smaller repeating patterns (centre left) with strong reds, greens and blues used in the earlier decade and more muted browns, beiges and orange in the later one. By the mid 1950s modern and exotic designs (centre right) in bolder colours were becoming acceptable although reproduction Regency designs (far right) had been popular since the end of the war. Paint also grew in popularity, especially as ready mixed colours became available off the shelf.*

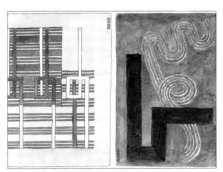

FIG 8.8: Flooring: *Carpet pieces and rugs were still widely used in this period, with some of the finest in bold, modern patterns like these Art Deco examples by Marion Dorn, while traditional designs remained popular throughout. Fitted carpets once again came into fashion towards the end of this period as prices dropped and vacuum cleaners became widely used.*

FIG 8.9: Fireplace surround: *The most distinctive feature of a 1930s interior was the tiled fireplace surround. Usually in beiges and browns with a stepped profile and a geometric pattern or emblem, it had either a matching coloured enamelled grate or, as in this example, a chrome electric bar heater.*

FIG 8.10: Door knobs: *Panelled doors with a full-width upper third and three vertical panels below or a series of horizontal ones were common in the 1930s, plain doors usually being fitted by the 1960s. Handles became fashionable in this period; Art Deco examples (above) were often in bronze, chrome or a hard white or brown plastic.*

FIG 8.11: Utility furniture: *Modern design in the interior was made more acceptable to the general public with the spread of utility furniture from the last years of the Second World War.*

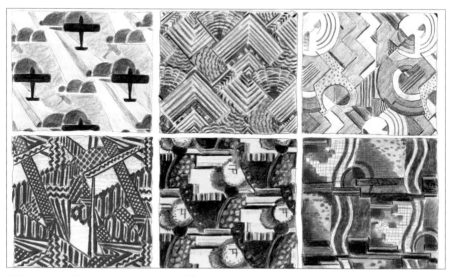

FIG 8.12 : Fabrics: *Art Deco-style fabrics with bold geometric patterns. Leading designers were influenced by Cubism, Ancient Egypt, the machine and the speed in creating these daring fabrics.*

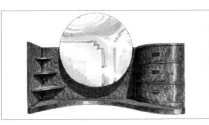

FIG 8.13: Bedrooms: *Bedrooms were lighter than those of the previous generation, with metal bedsteads and divans in most examples, and middle-class couples tending to have separate single beds until after the Second World War. Mass produced Art Deco bedroom furniture became widely available in the 1930s and complete suites were often bought in preference over new pieces for other rooms. This dresser top by the leading designer Betty Joel displays the new geometric and curving forms which could be created by using laminated woods.*

FIG 8.14: Bookcase: *Modernist designers, many of whom had fled Nazi Germany after 1933, began creating simple, functional and stylish furniture which although too avant-garde for most tastes would be highly influential after the war. This bookcase was designed by Jack Pritchard and Egon Riss while the former was in charge of Isokon in the late 1930s, a company which pioneered Modern design using laminated wood and steel and included work by leading German architects Walter Gropius and Marcel Breuer.*

FIG 8.15: Art Deco sideboards: *The earliest phase of Art Deco was characterised by richly-patterned surfaces, fine-quality marquetry, bronze-coloured detailing and luxurious fittings, with inspiration from Ancient Eygpt and new interpretations of Classical orders (left). By the 1930s, however, new materials, streamlined and curving forms and plain surfaces, some with chrome fittings and Bakelite handles, became fashionable.*

FIG 8.16: Art Deco dresser: *A characteristic 1930s-style dresser, with triple mirrors, rounded corners and stepped features.*

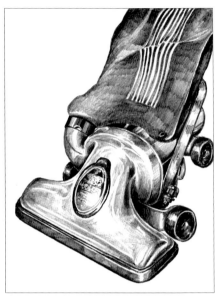

FIG 8.17: Vacuum cleaner: *New materials and modern design found acceptance within the home when used in electrical appliances. Vacuum cleaners like the Hoover pictured here made the task of having to shake and beat rugs and carpet pieces outside or laboriously brush them on hands and knees a thing of the past and helped make fitted carpets a practical option. This particular design was both functional and modern, using new materials like steel and plastic and making it both stylish and practical to maintain and repair.*

FIG 8.18: Radio: *It is hard to imagine evenings at home nowadays without television or music. When radio burst into the home in the inter war years, it was quite momentous and it seemed appropriate for this exciting and modern device to be styled in the latest Art Deco forms as in this example with its dynamic radiating vertical features and circular dial. Most mass-produced examples were made from Bakelite, a glossy, hard plastic which resembled wood and could easily be moulded into these fashionable forms.*

FIG 8.19: Light shades: *Electricity was now supplied to new housing, though used mainly for lighting and small appliances. In most houses solid fuel and gas provided heating and hot water although in some of the most modern flats flush-mounted wall heaters were the only source of warmth. Art Deco-style light fittings were popular with marble-effect glass bowls (see Fig 8.3), shades (top centre) and shell-like wall lights (bottom centre) being distinctive of the 1930s. Bronze-coloured fittings with stepped details and decorative clear glass shades (top right), standard lamps and some exotic styled pieces like this female figure table lamp (left) were also popular. By the 1950s straight lines and bold colours became fashionable as on this modern lamp (bottom right). Rough brush strokes and hand-drawn effect patterns were popular on wallpapers, fabrics and lampshades as in this example, inspired by a growing fashion for Continental living and Mediterranean styles.*

Glossary

Anaglypta:	From the Greek word meaning 'raised ornament', an embossed patterned wallpaper.
acanthus:	A leafy plant which was a popular Classical decorative form.
anthemion:	A honeysuckle leaf and flower design.
architrave/casing:	The moulded wooden or stone surround of a door or window.
Bakelite:	A hard plastic which could look like wood, named after its inventor L. H. Baekeland.
balusters:	Individual turned supports for a balustrade (supporting the rail up the side of stairs).
Baroque:	A Classical style with massive scale, deep features and rich ornamentation.
brocatelle:	A mixed woven fabric with a deep relief pattern.
barytides:	Human half figures.
chintz:	A glazed printed cotton fabric.
Classical order:	A style of Classical architecture which is most easily recognised by the style of the capital used on the columns.
Chinoiserie:	A French term for Chinese design and influence.
concave:	Inward curving surface.
convex:	Outward curving surface.
cornice:	A plain or decorative moulding around the top of a wall.
cretonne:	A heavy cotton upholstery or curtain fabric, often with floral pattern.
damask:	Originally a silk fabric from Damascus but now generally applied to a distinctive pattern of two dimensional stylised foliage.
egg and dart:	A decorative moulding with an egg shape divided up by the pointed end of a dart.
faux:	A French word for imitation.
fielded panel:	A panel with a raised central section with chamfered or angled sides.
fleur de lys:	A stylised iris flower design.
figured curl:	Wood with a swirling pattern.
fluted:	A column or pilaster with concave narrow grooves running vertically up it.
fretwork:	A geometric grid of interlacing lines formed into a band or panel.
frieze:	A large horizontal ornamental border along the top of a room or panelling.
herringbone:	A pattern formed from short angled pieces which appear like a horizontal zigzag. Used in brickwork, masonry and parquet flooring.
lambrequin:	A decorative piece of fabric draped across the top of curtains like a pelmet.
laminated wood/ plywood:	A board made from thin sheets of wood bonded together with the grain in opposite directions to make a strong and stable material used in furniture.
linoleum:	A flooring made from linseed oil, cork dust, wood flour and other ingredients set on a canvas backing (often called lino).
Lyncrusta:	A deeply embossed wallpaper.
marquetry:	Patterns in the surface of furniture made from different coloured inlaid wood.
Modernism:	In architecture it was a reaction against ancient styles and applied decoration from the early 20th century with simple shapes and ornamentation from the form of structure.
moire:	Fabric or wallpaper with a silky wood grain effect.
moulding:	An ornamental strip of wood or plaster with a decorative profile formed from concave, convex and angled elements.
muslin:	A loosely-woven cotton fabric.
newel post:	The end post of a balustrade on a staircase, often with a decorative finial on top.
palmette:	A stylised palm leaf motif.

parquet:	A geometric floor design formed from pieces of inlaid wood, often in short rectangles laid out in a herringbone pattern.
paterae:	Roman shallow, round dishes used for drinking.
Renaissance:	A rebirth of art, literature and learning based upon that of the Classical world across Europe from the 14th century. Its effects were not to be influential in Britain until the 16th century.
rep:	A wool or cotton fabric usually with a ribbed effect used for upholstery.
Rococo:	An asymmetrical and florid style of the mid 18th century, full of swirls, scrolls and shells, applied to plasterwork, carving and furniture and often in white and gold.
scroll:	An ornamental motif based on the end of a rolled up piece of paper or scroll.
size:	An adhesive-based mixture of varying thickness which is used to seal plaster walls and can form decoration.
strapwork:	A raised, flat decoration formed into lozenges and other geometric shapes which was popular on panelling and other carving in the late 16th and early 17th centuries.
Stucco:	A general term for a render which gained a bad reputation as it was often used to cover up poor building work in the late 18th and early 19th centuries.
swag:	An ornamental piece of fabric or garland draped between two points.
trompe l'oeil:	A painting effect used on ceilings and walls to make viewers think they are looking at a three-dimensional scene (a French term meaning 'fool the eye').
turned:	A rounded block of wood carved by rotating it while cutting a profile into it with a tool.

Useful websites

The internet is a rich resource of further information about specific details of the house interior. One area which is difficult to convey accurately in a book is the range of colours available. The following sites are useful as they contain paint cards, wallpaper or information about appropriate colours for a specific period:

http://wallpaperhistorysociety.org.uk
http://www.littlegreene.com/paint/colour/period-paint-colours
http://www.terracedhouses.co.uk/index5-paint.html
http://patrickbaty.co.uk
http://www.papers-paints.co.uk
http://www.bricksandbrass.co.uk
http://www.victoriansociety.org.uk

The Victoria and Albert Museum has a vast collection online, ranging from large pieces of furniture down to samples of fabric and wallpaper. These can be viewed at the following: http://collections.vam.ac.uk

Time Chart

NOTABLE ARCHITECTS AND DESIGNERS									

Notable Architects and Designers

─John Smythson
──── Robert Smythson ────
─Inigo Jones
─Robert Lyminge─

| 30 | 1540 | **1550** | 1560 | 1570 | 1580 | 1590 | **1600** | 1610 | 1620 | 16 |

TUDOR · ELIZABETHAN · JACOBEAN

TUDOR · **RENAISSANCE** (ELIZABETHAN PRODIGY HOUSE) · (JACOBEAN PRODIGY HOUSES)

── John Webb ──
──── Grinling Gibbons ────
Lord Burlington
── Hugh May ──
── Sir John Vanbrugh ──
── Sir Roger Pratt ──
── Nicholas Hawksmoor ──
James Gibbs ─

| 30 | 1640 | **1650** | 1660 | 1670 | 1680 | 1690 | **1700** | 1710 | 1720 | 17 |

JACOBEAN · COMMONWEALTH · RESTORATION · WILLIAM+MARY / ANNE · GEORGIAN

RENAISSANCE (CAROLEAN) · (DUTCH STYLE) · **BAROQUE**

William Kent
── George Hepplewhite ──
── Sir John Soane ──
── Thomas Sheraton ──
── Thomas Hope ─
── Thomas Chippendale ──
G. Leoni
── Thomas Shearer ──
── John Nash ──
── Robert Adam ──
── Sir William Chambers ──
─ Henry Holland ─

| 30 | 1740 | **1750** | 1760 | 1770 | 1780 | 1790 | **1800** | 1810 | 1820 | 18 |

GEORGIAN · REGENCY

PALLADIAN · **NEO-CLASSICISM** · PICTURESQUE / GOTHIC / NEO-CLASSICISM + GREEK REVIVAL

── Sir Charles Barry ──
── William Morris ──
E.W.Godwin
── Charles Rennie Mackintosh
── Richard Norman Shaw ──
A.W.N.Pugin ──
C.F.A. Voysey
John Loudon ── A.Salvin
── Philip Webb ──
── Sir Edwin Lutyens ──
Christopher Dresser

| 30 | 1840 | **1850** | 1860 | 1870 | 1880 | 1890 | **1900** | 1910 | 1920 | 19 |

VICTORIAN · EDWARDIAN · WWI MODERN

GOTHIC · ARTS+CRAFTS · TRADITIONALISTS
ITALIANATE · QUEEN ANNE · EDWARDIAN CLASSICISM

78

Index

Adams, Robert 27–29, 32
Art Deco 68–74
Art Nouveau 61, 66
Arts and Crafts 56–58, 61–66

Baillie Scott, M.H. 56, 57
balusters (balustrades) 8, 13, 15, 21, 22, 31, 38, 53, 68, 76
Baroque 15, 19, 76
bathrooms 47–49, 58, 59, 61
bedrooms/beds 7, 11, 13, 14, 19, 20, 37, 47, 48, 52, 55, 64, 73
bookcases 16, 23, 73

cabinets/sideboards 24, 27, 41, 54, 64, 69, 70, 73
carpets/rugs 5, 31, 43, 51, 64, 71
ceilings 5–10, 15, 30, 48, 58, 67, 69
chairs 11, 15, 17, 18, 25, 33, 37, 42, 43, 47, 54, 65, 69
Chinese/Chinoiserie 19, 25, 27, 31, 32
Chippendale, Thomas 19, 25, 32, 65
Classical style/orders 7, 8, 13–15, 19, 23, 27, 28, 36, 40, 43, 46, 57, 76
cornice 5, 18, 22, 31, 48, 51, 76
curtains 5, 30, 43, 48, 50, 52, 64

dado rail 5, 15, 18, 22, 27, 28, 37, 47, 50, 51, 57

dining rooms 21, 26-28, 36–38, 43, 47, 52, 54, 58, 68, 69
doors 7, 9, 14, 21, 38, 47, 53, 63, 72
drawing rooms 18, 21, 28, 36–38, 45, 47, 52, 58, 65

fabrics 6, 22, 30, 31, 43, 50, 52, 63, 64, 65, 72, 75
fireplaces 5–9, 14, 23, 29, 39, 47, 50, 52, 62, 69–71
floors 8, 31, 50, 51, 57, 64, 71
French/English Empire style 36, 40–42
frieze 5, 58, 61

Gibbons, Grinling 13
Gothic 7, 27, 31, 40, 46, 51, 52
grates 5, 29, 39, 53, 61, 62, 69

halls 7, 13, 14, 47, 56–58, 61, 68
Hepplewhite, George 32, 33, 40, 65

kitchens 13, 20, 36, 46, 49, 58, 59, 61, 64, 68, 70

library 21, 38, 43, 47
lighting 5, 34, 55, 66, 70, 75
living rooms 7, 13, 49, 67–69

Mackintosh, C.R. 62
mirrors 16, 24, 29, 41, 70

Modernism/Modernist 68, 72, 73, 76
Morris, William 46, 57, 61

paint /colours 6, 8, 22, 31, 38, 49, 58, 59, 61, 71
Palladian 19, 27
panelling 6, 8, 10, 14, 15, 22, 28, 47, 58
parlours 7, 13, 21, 49
pelmet 5, 30, 50, 64, 70
Pugin, A.W.N. 46
picture rail 5, 27, 51, 58, 69

ranges 39, 60, 70
Rococo 19, 23, 24, 25, 27, 51, 77

scullery 20, 46, 49, 60
Sheraton, Thomas 32, 34, 40, 65
skirting board 5, 31, 51, 69
sofas/settees 33, 37, 40, 43, 54
stairs 8–9, 15, 21, 31, 38, 53, 68, 69

tables 11, 16, 17, 24, 26–28, 32, 37, 40, 41, 47, 54
tiles 47, 50, 57, 61, 71
toilets 49–50, 59

Voysey, C.F.A. 57, 61, 64

wall hangings (tapestries) 6, 7, 22
wallpaper 22, 31, 38, 47,49, 57, 59, 61, 71, 75
windows 7, 14, 21, 36, 57, 59, 69

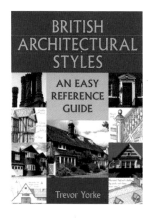

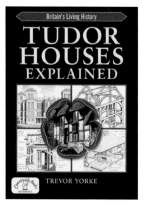

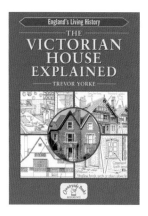

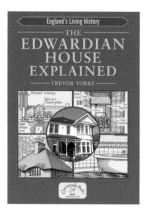

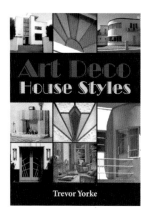

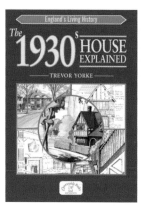

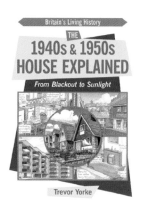